Solving Problems
Before They
Become Conflicts

Solving Problems Before They Become Conflicts

Norm Wakefield

PYRANEE
BOOKS

Zondervan Publishing House
Grand Rapids, Michigan

Solving Problems Before They Become Conflicts

Pyranee Books are published by the Zondervan Publishing House
1415 Lake Drive, S.E., Grand Rapids, Michigan 49506

Library of Congress Cataloging in Publication Data

Wakefield, Norm.
  Solving problems before they become conflicts.

    "Pyranee books"—T.p. verso.
    Bibliography: p.
    1. Interpersonal relations—Religious aspects—Christianity. I. Title.
BV4509.5.W33 1987   248.4   87-6164
ISBN 0-310-39091-5

All Scripture quotations, unless otherwise noted, are taken from the *Holy Bible:
New International Version* (North American Edition). Copyright © 1973, 1978,
1984, by the International Bible Society. Used by permission of Zondervan Bible
Publishers.

Verses marked TLB are from The Living Bible, copyright © 1971 by Tyndale
House Publishers, Wheaton, Illinois.

A note from the editor: In most general references in this book, the convention of
using male pronouns has been used. This has been done for the sake of simplicity.
The author and the editors realize that women and men are equally prone to conflict
and in need of the skills of problem solving.

Edited by John D. Sloan

Printed in the United States of America

87 88 89 90 91 / EE / 10 9 8 7 6 5 4 3 2 1

CONTENTS

Preface

This weekend I received a distressing phone call from a friend. Her raspy voice and tearful sobs told me that some tragedy had occurred. "Norm, we've called the wedding off. I've got pneumonia. The doctor says it will be two weeks before I'm well." She had called me to receive consolation and encouragement.

In a world filled with problems as well as joys, a moment of anticipation can turn into a moment of sadness. Those exciting wedding plans had to be scrapped for the moment so that something more urgent could be cared for.

This is the stuff of life—the unpredictable, the unmanageable, the sudden tragedy, the lurking disaster, the persistent nuisance, the gnawing problem, the unavoidable trial. But this is also the incredible challenge—the opportunity to be stretched, to be enriched, to discover, to explore, to grow.

Try as we may, we cannot escape difficulties. No one can. Even the newborn infant is thrust into a world of problems with which he must cope. He will face them until he dies. Yet this child—even our own children—doesn't get trained in how to solve problems. We say that our children must know how to read and write. We want our youngsters to be well-trained through college or vocational school. But how many of our sons and daughters are taught problem-solving skills? How many become skilled at this essential task? In my years of schooling from grade one to graduate school, I never had a course in basic problem solving, yet I have faced problems every day of my life.

This book focuses on solving problems, the problems that

occur between people or that face individuals. Many problems arise that we face alone, but some of the most painful ones are those that we share with others. Some of our saddest memories center on broken friendships, severed relationships, divorced families.

I believe that healthy understanding about problems and trials comes from our biblical insights. I am convinced that a strong, genuine confidence in God's power, compassion, and wisdom is vital to effective problem solving. It is the taproot that gives us strength to cope with the unpredictable, the painful, the difficult. And so I have attempted to base the issues in this book on a theology of God's nature.

Many people have contributed to this book. I am especially grateful for the individuals who have encouraged me to develop these ideas in my seminars and retreats. Others' feedback has helped my ideas mature.

One new experience this book has provided is working with my daughter Amy. She and I brainstormed the PERSONAL DISCOVERY and PERSONAL FEEDBACK sections at the end of each chapter; then I wrote them. It has been a most enjoyable father-daughter experience.

My family has consistently encouraged me in my writing projects. I am grateful to my wife, Winnie, and my five children for their support.

I also want to express my appreciation to Linda Lierman, who read the manuscript and offered constructive evaluation of my grammar.

After I had written six chapters, Ed and Vi Janos said they wanted to encourage my writing by providing a computer with a word-processor program. That gift has made my task much easier and more efficient. I am grateful for their confidence in me and their investment in my ministry.

Above all, I am grateful to the Lord for the opportunity to write. My prayer is that this book will honor Him and encourage others. I remember where the Lord found me; any credit must go to Him.

PART I
INTRODUCTION

Chapter One

HOW PROBLEMS CAN BECOME YOUR FRIENDS

The most important principle of this book is that *conflict is a mismanaged problem.* Conflict arises when we neglect problem solving, or we use defective or ineffective problem-solving procedures.

I have written this book to examine this premise and demonstrate three of its implications.

First, the statement *conflict is a mismanaged problem* implies that problems are our friends, not our enemies. We could never become healthy, productive individuals without problems, trials, or challenges to face. We would have no way to develop healthy "muscle tone" (physically, mentally, socially, emotionally, or spiritually) if we never confronted obstacles. Imagine a child that experienced a problem-free environment. Such an environment would be a curse rather than a blessing because it would seriously inhibit his growth. J. C. Penny is reported to have said:

> I am grateful for all my problems. As each of them was overcome I became stronger and more able to meet those yet to come. I grew on all my difficulties.

We give children puzzles as gifts. A puzzle is a problem to be solved. It is an opportunity to hunt, discriminate, perceive, try out, question, or ponder. The simplest childhood puzzle is a picture of all the problems we will face in our lifetime. The apostle James was so convinced of the value of trials (adult puzzles) that he said a healthy Christian will consider them joy.[1]

A second implication of the principle about problems and conflicts is that conflict is unhealthy. Examine the root meaning of the word and you'll see why. The word is derived from the Latin word *conflictus*, which indicates the "act of striking together." The dictionary uses such words as "antagonistic state or action," "hostile encounter," "fight, battle, war," and "collision."[2]

Conflict at its core means striking out at others with conscious or unconscious intent to injure or destroy. Conflict involves painfully destructive behavior that is detrimental to people and to productive problem solving. Read the comments of Seifert and Clinebell.

> However necessary conflict may be, there is always a price tag attached . . . especially when conflict is an expression of self-centered interests, it contradicts the thrust of Christian love, which is to maximize gains for other persons. . . . Psychologically and socially, conflict is also costly. There are psychological perils in exaggerated ego strivings. Personality damage easily follows a breakdown in relationships. Any social struggle is dangerous to both winners and losers, involving temptations respectively to arrogance and to resentment.[3]

We commonly use the words "problem" and "conflict" as synonyms. This lack of distinction is confusing and stops us from seeing the basic difference in the two processes. It also keeps us from discovering the positive process of problem solving and from tossing out the destructive process of conflict. Claiming conflict is good opens up the way to justifying destructive actions as mere "problem solving."

A third implication of my premise is that effective problem solving is a healthy, positive experience that can be undertaken in a thoughtful, skillful manner. It is a learned behavior based upon healthy attitudes. Unfortunately, few of us were carefully trained to be skilled problem solvers. We travel through life trying to work through problems without the practical know-how. Making the task more painful with each encounter, we bump, bruise, and wound each other.

PROBLEMS OR PEOPLE?

Let's attack one more issue that is basic to this book: *The root issue is not problems but people.* We've already seen that problems are an invaluable ingredient to our growth and development. Without them we would be handicapped.

The real issue is that people approach problems in different ways. They bring anger, fear, distrust, and a variety of other emotions that muddy the water. They often are tired, confused, or uninformed so they cannot think clearly. They have little or no knowledge and skill of the problem-solving process; therefore, they cannot deal with the problem constructively. The result, conflict.

To illustrate what I'm saying, let's look at an incident from the Bible. The narrative is recorded in 1 Samuel 25.

David was a fugitive from King Saul. He had been hiding in the desert of Maon with six hundred of his men. Since he had to keep on the move, he had no way to secure food for his band of followers. He depended on people in the area to be generous. Word was brought that a wealthy man, Nabal, was shearing sheep. Since David's men had provided protection for Nabal's shepherds, David believed it was appropriate to ask for food. He sent ten of his men to Nabal with the request.

Approach 1: Nabal

To understand how Nabal copes with problems, we need to know more about him. What is he like? What kind of underlying attitudes motivate his actions? In 1 Samuel 25:3, we discover a valuable clue. The writer states that Nabal was a surly man, suggesting he related to people in a rude, thoughtless manner. His response to problems came from a hardened heart.

It also says that Nabal was "mean in his dealings." His unfeeling heart dictated how he would relate to other people. The men who were sent by David came in a courteous, thoughtful manner and were treated with a belligerent spirit. Notice that Nabal didn't bother to seek valuable facts. His question "Who is this David?" was not asked to gain perspective; rather, it came as an insult, suggesting that Nabal was an irresponsible, rebellious troublemaker. If he had taken the time to question the servant who spoke to his wife Abigail, he would have seen his faulty perspective.

One of Nabal's own men gave a fascinating commentary about his leader: "He is such a wicked man that no one can talk with him" (v. 17). In fact, he "hurled insults" at David's messengers (v. 14).

The Nabal approach doesn't solve problems; it leads to disastrous conflicts. Be rude. Be sarcastic. Be closed-minded. Reap disaster.

Nabal's response represents an approach that is painful to people. Nabals solve their problems by manipulating, overpowering, intimidating, and controlling others. Their approach is that of a foolish person (v. 25) and leads to conflict, disaster, death.

Approach 2: David

Let's examine David's problem-solving approach. He faced the problem in a logical, thoughtful manner: "My men are hungry. How shall I feed them?" As he was pondering this dilemma, he realized that he had provided security for Nabal's shepherds and that it should be worth something.

David's approach was courteous. He instructed his messengers to speak in a friendly, positive manner. It's as if David said, "Tell Nabal I wish him the best of health and prosperity."

David recognized that Nabal might need additional information. "He may not know of the protection we have generously provided. He may not know that we are honest, trustworthy people." David invited Nabal to seek out further information from reliable sources—his own servants (v. 8).

David's initial approach to problem solving was healthy, positive, and constructive. But notice what happened as stage two unfolded.

His men returned empty-handed. They gave their report of Nabal's abusive behavior.

How did David respond?

First, he acted prematurely. There is no evidence that he took time to think, pray, or seek counsel from others. Instead, he reacted impulsively to a negative situation.

Second, he acted rashly, responding with deep-rooted, strong negative emotions. He was willing to destroy innocent people for one man's insensitivity. He had not considered that all of Nabal's clan were not like their leader.

Third, he acted offensively. He barked, "Put on your swords!" (v. 13). Fight! Attack! Destroy! Get even! When David's solution to the problem was rejected, he allowed destructive emotions, which would lead to tragic conflict, to overpower him. Innocent people would weep; no one would be the same again.

This approach to problems is typical of individuals who come to others with good intentions. They mean well and try to create a positive setting. But when their initial good will is rejected, they allow negative emotions to arise and overpower constructive, clear thinking. Then solutions are forced into a setting of conflict. Frequently, it leads to the death of a relationship or seriously wounded friendships.

Approach 3: Abigail

Thankfully, there was a person who acted to avert an impending disaster. Her practical wisdom is worth exploring for our enrichment.

She listened to wise counsel. Here is a distinguishing mark between this lady and her husband. The servant said of

Nabal, "No one can talk with him" (v. 17). Yet he knew he could come to Abigail, express alarming concern, and receive a hearing. Abigail recognized the wisdom of the servant's words and lost no time in acting upon them. *She was intelligent* (v. 3). The two qualities that are used to describe Abigail are intelligent and beautiful. Although women are frequently typed as emotional and beautiful, here Abigail witnessed to God's enabling both men and women to act in wise, knowledgeable ways to resolve difficult issues. Abigail's response may encourage today's women to observe that it was a woman who delivered two emotion-bound men from disaster by her clear, thoughtful resolution of the dilemma.

None of the three actors in this narrative was superior to the other. Each had *learned* to cope with situations through various life situations. Nabal and David *learned* to face problems in unhealthy ways. (This is not to say that David always solved problems poorly.) Each had learned to give way to hostile emotions. Abigail must have felt fear and disgust, but she didn't allow these emotions to overpower intelligent, logical thought.

She initiated positive action (vv. 18–19). Abigail swiftly gathered a variety of foods, mobilized her servants to pack supplies on donkeys, and hastened to meet David. She wisely realized that David's hostile actions would be thwarted more quickly by food than by words. Her actions were not directed toward an unreasonable husband. She sought out the most critical problem, attacked it, and did not attract other needless problems while she concentrated on solving it.

She acted with humility (v. 23). When Abigail encountered David, she assumed a physical position of humility by bowing to the ground at his feet. Her words, too, were words of respect and humility: "My lord . . . your servant" (v. 24).

This lady's behavior is amazing in two ways. First, it

stands in direct contrast to the arrogance and pride seen in Nabal and David. Neither would have humbled himself before the other. Second, Abigail's humility comes from strength, not weakness. The context suggests that she was acting wisely to resolve a potentially explosive situation. The entire passage portrays her strength of character.

One of the key elements in keeping problems from escalating to conflicts is the spirit of humility. A willingness to say "I may be wrong," "I need to learn from you," or "Your solution is best" communicates a cooperative spirit of good will, which aids the other person in laying down his weapons.

She took a defenseless position. The courage, strength, and wisdom seen in Abigail is impressive. Her words "Let the blame fall on me alone" are noteworthy. Not only did she avoid David's attacking Nabal, she also was willing to accept responsibility in a benevolent way. She did not plead her innocence; she did not criticize David's actions—she defused the situation with her nonhostile strength.

She helped David see his advantage in nonconflict (vv. 26–31). Abigail reminded David of the cost of violence. She challenged him to allow God to be the avenger of another's wickedness. She reminded him of the priceless gift of a clear conscience. While the reader might see this as manipulative strategy on Abigail's part, the important point is that she was causing him to remember God's truth and principles he cherished.

How often in our skirmishes we come away feeling guilty because of careless words we uttered in a heated moment. We feel cheap and unchristian because we have angrily and unfairly attacked another. What a gift of grace—to protect others from the scars of conflict by our humility, love, and wisdom.

She defused David's violent anger (vv. 32–34). Before this remarkable lady arrived, David was eager to slaughter every man in Nabal's household. After he experienced her redemptive actions, he cried out, "Praise be to the Lord, the God of Israel, who has sent you today to meet me." Before Abigail appeared, he was anticipating murder; after, he was praising God.

Abigail symbolizes the strength of godliness that leads to effective problem solving. While the challenge of this book is to learn problem-solving skills, an even greater challenge is to become women and men who can live fully within the Spirit's resources, so the fruit of grace, love, and wisdom influence our problems, trials, and stressful encounters.

Personal Discovery

1. I have said that problems and conflicts are not the same: Problems are good; conflict is bad. Do you agree or disagree? Jot down your own thoughts.

2. The narrative in 1 Samuel 25 gives us three examples of how people face problems. It is helpful to see them in "flesh and blood." I'd like you to review each of the examples (Nabal, David, and Abigail) and then identify someone you know who faces problems similarly. You are not doing this to condemn others, but as an effort to identify someone you know who uses this approach. Don't reveal names, but write a description of how each behaves.

A "Nabal" I know:

A "David" I know:

An "Abigail" I know:

3. Seven positive problem-solving qualities were found in Abigail. List any of these that you would like to strengthen in your life. Begin to pray regularly for God to show you ways you can grow in this area(s).

Personal Feedback
(Discussion questions I can think through with family members, friends, or work associates.)

1. Discuss whether you are more afraid of people, problems, or both? Can you determine why?

2. Talk about how your personal background has influenced your attitude and actions toward problems and conflicts. How did your parents cope with problems? Share any significant events that shaped your ideas and attitudes about problem solving or conflict.

3. Most people would like to strengthen themselves in the seven qualities noted in Abigail. Imagine someone came to you and asked for ideas to practice to grow stronger. See if you can come up with at least two suggestions for each of the seven areas.

Chapter Two

HOW PROBLEMS AND CONFLICTS DIFFER

In 1947, *Harper's Magazine* published a fascinating short story by John Bell Clayton entitled "The White Circle." The opening paragraph thrusts us into the center of a developing conflict between two boys, Tucker and Anvil. The event is seen through twelve-year-old Tucker's eyes.

> As soon as I saw Anvil squatting up in the tree like some hateful creature that belonged in trees I knew I had to take a beating and I knew the kind of beating it would be. But still I had to let it be that way because this went beyond any matter of courage or shame.
>
> The tree was mine. [1]

Anvil had violated Tucker's personal territory, because he had perched himself in an apple tree that Tucker owned. Tucker's immediate response destines that the situation will become a conflict rather than a problem. Notice how he perceived the scene and how what he said invites hostility from Anvil.

> . . . the tree was mine and now there perched Anvil, callously munching one of my thirteen apples and stowing the rest inside his ragged shirt until it bulged out in ugly lumps. I knew the apples pressed cold against his hateful belly and to me the coldness was a sickening evil.
>
> I picked up a rock out of the dust of the road and tore across the creek bed and said, "All right, Anvil—climb down! [2]

Clayton's vivid account of this emerging conflict reminds us how early in life difficult situations we have to solve confront us. Within a few short years, we have established our personal strategy to face the world, its obstacles and opportunities. For many children, the callous, perhaps careless, way adults relate to them effectively programs conflict into their lifestyles when they are quite young.

> There were times when I had no desire to kill Anvil. I remember the day his father showed up at the school. He was a dirty, half-crazy, itinerant knick-knack peddler. He had a club and told the principal he was going to beat the meanness out of Anvil or kick him to death. Anvil scudded under a desk and lay there trembling and whimpering until the principal finally drove the ragged old man away.[3]

How powerfully this young lad's life had been marred by a violent father. He destined his son to be a vengeful child, striking out at those he could control.

The patterns of problem-solving behavior and conflict behavior are significantly different. We can quickly perceive the approaching storm of conflict in the opening sentences of Clayton's story. In like manner, we can identify the characteristics of the problem solver, as we observe him in action if we were to continue reading the story. Our task in this chapter is to distinguish between problem solving and conflict.

HOW PROBLEM SOLVING AND CONFLICT DIFFER

The perceptive observer will see at least six differences between a problem-solving approach and a conflict-arousing approach. Before looking at these differences, however, I want to observe that many situations are combinations of problem-solving behavior and conflict behavior. Let me suggest three reasons for this mixing of behaviors.

First, people often begin to discuss problems in a positive

manner, but the process deteriorates into a conflict encounter. Thus, we will observe both kinds of behavior. (The incident of David described in chapter one is an example.) Second, because at least two individuals are involved, one may be using a problem-solving approach; the other, a conflict approach. Third, when conflict has run its course and emotions are vented, individuals may turn to a more constructive approach to cope with the difficulty.

With these considerations in mind, let's examine the primary differences between problem solving and conflict. *Problem solving is a constructive process; conflict is a destructive process.* Ideally, problem solving is a commitment by two or more individuals to work together in a positive spirit toward a solution that benefits all. There may be differences, tension, even impasses; however, we can approach them with an attitude of courtesy, respect, and good will and work through them in a positive manner. The outcome is healthy, beneficial, and constructive.

Not so with conflict.

Conflict destroys, tears down, wastes. When conflict erupts, be ready for six negative outcomes:

Watch valuable energy being wasted. Emotional energy gets poured down the drain, so to speak, and leaves people physically exhausted.

Watch relationships being damaged or destroyed. Watch unity evaporate. Twice the energy will be needed to heal the hurts or repair the damage.

Watch problems become enmeshed with complications, diversions, and roadblocks. Watch the problems be left unsolved.

Watch creativity waste away. Observe ideas become rigid, defensive, dogmatic. Watch the death of creativity.

Watch self-confidence erode. With each recurrence, you will detect more doubt and a lower self-esteem. So often, conflicts leave us feeling cheap, dirty, defeated.

Watch God's honor be attacked by our unchristian behavior. Rather than "They will know you are Christians by your love," it will be "They will wonder if you are Christians by your anger, your fighting, your sarcasm, your attacks."

Some contemporary writers advocate fighting to solve problems. Edward Ford has this to say about fighting:

A big problem in some marriages is fighting. Some say that fighting is good. "It clears the air," they say. Others claim this type of ventilation helps to get it "out of your system." Don't believe it! Fighting always hurts! It leads to exaggeration and distortion. The only thing you learn from fighting is how to fight. *Fighting is the bottom of the negative spectrum* [emphasis mine].[4]

Ford calls fighting "super negative behavior." I agree. It contains the seeds of harshness, which can only stir up strife (Prov. 15:1). In most situations, it will leave the problem unsolved at a high cost to interpersonal relationships. Fighting, a form of conflict behavior, is a destructive process.

Problem solving focuses on an issue "for" the people involved; conflict focuses on an issue "between" the people involved. The symbols in figures A and B visualize the difference.

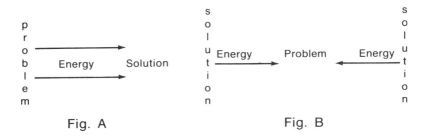

Fig. A   Fig. B

Figure A represents a problem-solving approach. The

arrows are symbolic of two individuals who recognize a problem they share. Together they focus their energy on a wiser solution than either has within himself. Figure B represents a conflict approach. The problem separates two individuals. Each approaches it with his predetermined answer, so the encounter quickly becomes a tense standoff, which involves quarreling and strife. Each fights for his solution. Energy is expended against each other, rather than toward the problem. And each person consumes a considerably higher volume of energy in conflict behavior than in problem-solving behavior.

Problem solving prompts healthy reactions; conflict prompts hyper-reactions. Problem solvers are people with emotions— the same emotions as individuals prone to conflict. They experience anger and disappointment. They have solutions that appeal to them. They fear what some solutions will cost them, or do to them.

The difference is not in emotions; it is in the intensity of reactions. The problem solver requires his emotions to live under the discipline of love and clear thinking, whereas a person given to conflict allows emotional responses to lead the way and dictate the solution.

Observe how the following proverbs state the matter.

"A fool is quick-tempered; a wise man stays cool when insulted" (12:16, TLB).

"Self-control means controlling the tongue! A quick retort can ruin everything" (13:3, TLB).

"A wise man controls his temper. He knows that anger causes mistakes" (14:29, TLB).

Problem solvers *do* have emotions. The key is that they have learned constructive ways to deal with their emotions, so as not to cloud clear thinking and so as not to create a setting that is destructive or inflaming to the other person. For example, they are convinced that a gentle response is more helpful than a harsh response if another person is upset, so they choose the more helpful response. *Problem solving keeps the problem as the focus; conflict keeps the self as the focus.* The problem solver honestly wants both persons to win. He believes that in the majority of situations a solution exists that is beneficial for all persons involved. The problem solver commits himself to work with the other person to discover that answer to the dilemma. The truth of Proverbs 18:15 is his banner: "The heart of the discerning acquires knowledge; the ears of the wise seek it out."

A problem-solving approach creates a stronger bond of trust between persons. When I know that others are not trying to manipulate, exploit, or belittle me, I am more motivated to be open and positive in seeking a solution. A more relaxed, constructive setting is possible. Em Griffin observes that "paradoxically, we have the most influence on people when we are the least manipulative."[5]

The environment in conflict is noticeably different. "I want my way!" is the dominant message. "You are bad," "Your way is stupid," "You're to blame" are accompanying emphases. Conflict behavior is "I" win. Truthfully, most conflict is an exercise in selfishness—an exercise in noncaring, nonlistening, nonlove—that may have been learned subconsciously over a period of years. This book is a challenge to begin dealing honestly with these destructive patterns through the power of God and a commitment to growth.

Problem-solving stresses rational thinking processes; conflict stresses irrational thinking processes. In chapter one, I observed that Abigail's intelligence was a dominant quality. Her clear, logical approach to a dangerous problem provided a solution that averted disaster. Nabal and David's approaches were heavily loaded with illogical, emotionally charged thinking that spelled disaster.

All too often, conflict issues are prompted by underlying motives, emotions, or issues that the individual has lost sight

of, or never knew existed in the first place. The root issue
may have begun many years ago. Psychologist John Quesnell, writing about conflict in marriage, states:

> The thousands of couples I have seen in marital therapy and
> weekend seminars have demonstrated to me that many
> disagreements in marriage have little or nothing to do with
> present reality. A couple may disagree about finances, visits
> with in-laws, etc. After a moment of discussion, the initial
> focus of the disagreement is lost and the couple find
> themselves enmeshed in a frustrating system of interaction in
> which they cannot specifically identify the central issues
> involved in their dispute. [6]

Two other important differences related to thinking
processes and problem solving should be mentioned. Problem solvers make more use of divergent thinking processes;
conflict producers center on convergent thinking processes.
Divergent thinking seeks as many solutions as possible.
"Let's see if we can find ten possible ways this problem
could be solved." The convergent thinker says, "There's
only one solution to the problem." (And almost always it is
his solution, made to *his* advantage.) He uses a closed-mind
approach, which is highly unproductive.

The second difference basic to how problem solvers and
conflict producers think is this: Problem solvers are creative
thinkers; conflict producers are unimaginative. Effective
solutions result from open-ended, nonjudgmental thinking.
New, insightful ways are discovered that neither party has
envisioned before they combined their energies.

*Problem solving more likely leads to an effective, healthy
solution; conflict more likely leads to unresolved problems, or a
solution forced on one person.* Each of the five previous
problem-solving characteristics contributes to quality solutions, ones that benefit both individuals. This last distinction
emphasizes that the fruit of this approach is pleasing for all
people involved in the process. Both solutions and relationships are enhanced.

Conflict bears bitter fruit. Not only are the solutions likely to be poorer, the motivation to implement them is much less. The relationships are weakened, if not destroyed, and even the "winner" becomes a loser.

He loses his own respect because he has manipulated, overpowered, or intimidated another.

He loses the respect of others whom he needs.

He loses the other person's energy and enthusiasm to implement the solution.

He loses the opportunity to discover a better, more creative way.

He loses the chance to enrich, build up, affirm the other person.

AN EXPENSIVE LOSS! In the wisdom of the Proverbs we read, "The fool who provokes his family to anger and resentment will finally have nothing worthwhile left. He shall be the servant of a wiser man" (Prov. 11:29, TLB).

We can now see why problem solving and conflict must be seen as two distinct processes. To think of them as one and the same is a mistake that compounds the problem. Only as we see them separately, can we build a healthy model. In the remaining chapters of this book, I will endeavor to keep the two processes separate.

Personal Discovery

1. In chapter one's *Personal Discovery,* I asked you to do some preliminary thinking about the difference between problems and conflicts. In this chapter, I have detailed several important differences. It is vital that you integrate the information from this chapter with your thoughts from the previous one. Doing this will help you further clarify your own thoughts about problems and conflict.

Ask yourself, "Do I agree or disagree with the distinction between problems and conflicts that chapter two makes?" If you disagree, write down *facts* to support your position.
2. The Book of Proverbs has much to say about individuals who are "problem-centered" and those who are "conflict-centered." Look up the three verses under each heading below and write down the characteristic identified.

Problem-Oriented Person	Conflict-Oriented Person
15:23	17:19
17:27	18:2
20:5	18:13

If you feel motivated to pursue this study further, I have chosen several more verses that will allow you to enrich your profile of these two types of individuals. (Or you may want to read through Proverbs and do a complete study of the "problem-oriented" person and the "conflict-oriented" person.) 1:5; 4:1; 10:12, 19, 32; 11:12; 12:15, 18; 13:3; 15:1, 4, 18; 16:21; 17:14; 19:19, 20; 21:19; 22:10; 24:29; 25:15; 26:18, 19, 24, 25; 28:13; 29:2.

3. Review the six distinctions made in this chapter between problems and conflicts. On the basis of those distinctions *and* the data you've written down for exercise two, are you problem-oriented or conflict-oriented? Write down several reasons to support your answer.

4. Think of a conflict situation that you have experienced recently. Write down the situation. Now list the emotional, mental, and physical results of the conflict. How could the outcome of this situation have differed if a problem-solving approach had been used?

Personal Feedback

1. Discuss your agreement or disagreement with the distinctions made in this chapter. (One problem-solving skill is learning to discuss differences without becoming disagreeable—trying to learn from each other's insights and also trying to distinguish facts from opinions.)

2. Imagine that you are a counselor. Individuals come to you for help in reducing their conflict behavior. Talk about the ideas you would suggest for each person who is seeking help.

   Person #1: "I'm always so defensive. I feel like I'm being attacked."

   Person #2: "I'm a very emotional person. When problems arise I get excited and irrational. My husband says, 'Don't get so hyper.'"

   Person #3: "People tell me I'm too negative. I always find what's wrong with an idea, or why it won't work. Then they get depressed."

   Person #4: "When problems arise, I feel as though I have to win. I'm very competitive. I'll argue even when I know I'm wrong."

3. Describe to each other the most effective problem solver you know. Identify the distinguishing characteristics that make that person a successful problem solver.

PART II
BIBLICAL ROOTS FOR PROBLEM SOLVING

Chapter Three

FINDING GOD IN
YOUR PROBLEMS

To introduce an important truth, I want you to participate in an "imagining" activity. I will sketch four scenes for you. After each scene, read what you are to do, then pause, close your eyes, and try to sense the feelings you would experience in the situation.

Scene 1: Imagine yourself as an eight-year-old child. You are standing alone in front of your class at school. Your teacher is glaring at you. She accuses you—remember you are before the entire class—of cheating on an exam. Her accusations burn like a branding iron; you sting with humiliation. She says finally, "You and I are going to the principal's office. He has ways to deal with cheaters!"

Close your eyes for a few moments and imagine how you would feel. What specific emotions would you experience? What would you want to do?

Scene 2: Imagine the same setting as scene 1, the same accusation, the same hostile teacher; however, someone is standing beside you—the most compassionate, understanding father you can imagine. You know that he loves you unconditionally and is there to be with you through this difficult experience. You feel him reach out and take your hand, then hold it firmly, yet gently.

Close your eyes for a few moments and imagine how you would feel in this second scene. How would your feelings differ from scene 1? What would you want to do?

Scene 3: Imagine that you are a thirty-eight-year-old

person. Your boss has called you before the rest of the employees. He accuses you of stealing $1,500 from the company funds. His words are sarcastic and threatening. Finally, he says, "I have notified the police and they are on their way here to arrest you."

As you close your eyes again, imagine what feelings you would experience. What would you want to do?

Scene 4: Imagine the same setting as scene 3; however, standing beside you is your strong, compassionate, understanding heavenly Father. In your spirit you feel Him reach out and take your hand.

How would your feelings differ in scene 3 and scene 4? How would your responses differ?

THE REALITY OF A LOVING FATHER

The "imagining" activity raises a key issue. How do we face problems and trials? Do we cope with them independently, that is, do we try to find adequate resources within ourselves for every situation? Or, do we experience an amazing partnership with an eternal, intimate Father who shares all of life's experiences with us? To what extent is the Lord an active, loving, supportive strength within your life, empowering you to face the smallest or the greatest problem confidently?

As long as I'm posing a number of questions, let me ask another strategic one: What comes to your mind when you think of God? The most important issue that influences successful problem solving is our experiential relationship with the Lord.

Will we . . .

   commit our problems to the Lord if we don't really trust Him?

   find strength from the Lord if we have no sense of intimacy with Him?

rest peacefully in difficult situations if we're afraid He is indifferent or incompetent?

release anger against someone if we're not confident God is in control?

come to the Lord for counsel and direction if we believe that He is a harsh, celestial bully?

bring our problems to the Lord if we fear He will choose the meanest solutions to prove He is boss?

cry out to Him if we're not sure He listens?

I recall a person sitting in my office who was discouraged about her relationship with the Lord. I asked, "Do you experience the same feelings with Jesus as you do with the heavenly Father?" "Oh, no, I feel much closer to Jesus. It's God the Father that always seems so stern, so disapproving." This person has been a Christian for over thirty years, yet has always known the Lord as a harsh, demanding Father.

A. W. Tozer accurately perceived that "the man who comes to a right belief about God is relieved of ten thousand temporal problems, for he sees at once that these have to do with matters which at most cannot concern him very long."[1]

As I prepared myself to write this book, I began to see even more clearly that one of the most powerful themes throughout the Bible is the importance of the trials, problems, and struggles person after person faced. Many turned to the Lord in these difficult events and found His strength, His wisdom, His protection, His refreshment, His grace, His deliverance. Others relied on their own strength and found defeat, sorrow, and death. The witness of the Word of God is sobering.

God has called us to new life in Jesus Christ. We have been brought into "the kingdom of the Son he loves."[2] As citizens of the eternal kingdom, the Lord is cultivating a new lifestyle within us, an eternal way of thinking and behaving. He wants us to share His very nature. I am convinced that you may pass over this matter too quickly. Think about this: The problems we face throughout life—large and small—are *deliberately* there to cause us to turn to our Father, to discover the experiential reality of all that the Scriptures teach about Him. The tragedy for most of us is that we encounter problems and cope with them in our own strength, or we rely upon others when we should turn to God. Either way, we never discover the fullness of His power, His intimacy, His wisdom, His love. Rather than being more fully prepared to walk with Him, we continue to build our lives around our own sufficiency.

The Bible illustrates this point powerfully as it introduces us to individual after individual who discovers the reality of God when he turns to Him in time of need. Let's consider two examples.

Joseph

Probably no one in the Old Testament encountered more problems than Joseph, son of Jacob. We are hardly introduced to him before he was in trouble with his brothers. Serious trouble! He barely escaped being murdered when he was sold into slavery. Then he was falsely accused of rape and tossed into prison. He assisted a fellow prisoner, yet when the other man was released, he forgot Joseph. He faced one problem after another!

Three observations from Scripture put Joseph's problems in perspective. First, a revealing statement about Joseph and God was made and repeated as Joseph encountered problem upon problem: "The Lord was with Joseph and he prospered;"[3] "The Lord was with Joseph and He gave him success in whatever he did."[4] Joseph experienced God's presence and prosperity *in the midst* of problems. The trials were the context in which God's reality became genuine.

Second, Joseph realized the plan of God being worked out through his struggles. He perceived that even injustices done against him were used for God's ultimate good purposes. He declared this to his brothers.

> "Do not be distressed and do not be angry with yourselves for selling me here, because it was to save lives that *God sent me ahead* of you. For two years now there has been famine in the land, and for the next five years there will not be plowing and reaping. But *God sent me ahead* of you to preserve for you a remnant on earth and save your lives by a great deliverance.

> "So then, it was not you who sent me here, but *God. He made me father to Pharoah,* lord of his entire household and ruler of all Egypt. Now hurry back to my father and say to him, 'This is what your son Joseph says: *God has made me* lord of all Egypt.' "5

What incredible perception Joseph possessed. What clear, powerful insight he passes on to us. Not only is the Almighty a present reality, He is also using the most difficult situations to accomplish significant purposes in a person's life.

A third lesson from Joseph's life gives us insight. Joseph's problems were an essential part of his life preparation. Too often we see troubles as isolated incidents or chance happenings. It is hard to perceive them as deliberate training events designed to bring about deeper faith in Jesus Christ, purer holiness of purpose, or stronger commitment to Him. The writer of Hebrews reminds us that God's disciplining process can train us in a life of godliness; its fruit will be the peaceful fruit of righteousness. At the time, it is painful; seen in long-term perspective, it is invaluable. 6

Paul

In the Book of Philippians, we find Paul confined to a jail cell. Miserable living conditions, inhuman treatment, wretched food, no freedom!

Strangely enough he mentioned none of these in his letter to the Philippian Christians. Rather, his epistle was saturated with joy and optimism at what God was achieving through this "problem" situation. The perceptive reader cannot miss Paul's genuine excitement about fellow believers being strengthened, prison guards discovering life in Christ, and fellow leaders preaching the gospel more boldly.

Paul reminds us of Joseph. His God-centered perspective made a basic difference in how he saw his condition. Where others only found a reason to complain, Paul found a reason to rejoice.

GOD-CENTERED PERCEPTION OF PROBLEMS

Joseph and Paul are two witnesses among scores recorded in the Scriptures. Each clearly identifies what happens when problems are handled alone and what happens when they are handled together with God. The Bible emphatically states by example after example that God allows us to encounter problems—big, small, medium-sized, long-term, short-term—to help us discover fullness of life in Him. They are the most practical way to find the power of His indwelling life. Consistently discovering God's way of handling problems transforms us with new power, new perception, and new purpose.

My research for this book has led me to an exciting discovery. I found that numerous aspects of God's nature directly relate to how we face and solve problems. Within the very essence of who He is are abundant resources to handle problems successfully.

Christians commonly speak of having a "personal relationship" with Jesus Christ; numerous biblical verses affirm that Jesus Christ lives within us. Second Peter 1:4 makes the powerful statement that we "participate in the divine nature." If we are privileged to have this remarkable identity with the living God, then why shouldn't we be able to solve any problem through the resources of who He is?

The next six chapters examine specific characteristics of God's nature and reveal how these influence problem solving. Each characteristic has a significant relationship to all of us Christians and how we can cope with problems.

Part II is unquestionably the heart of this book. God's indwelling presence and power make the difference in the Christian's problem-solving posture. Being a Christian in no way guarantees us that life will be easier or more "successful." Being a Christian does guarantee each of us an inseparable link with the absolute Resource that can empower us in any circumstance.

Personal Discovery

1. The way we relate to our heavenly Father is often rooted in our relationship with our earthly father. For many, this leads to a distorted image of their heavenly Father. It is important to evaluate the impact of our earthly father's example on our understanding of, and relationship to, our heavenly Father. The following exercises will help you evaluate your father-child relationships.

   A. List all the ways you think your earthly father is *similar to* your heavenly Father. Make a second list that tells all the ways your earthly father is *unlike* your heavenly Father.

   B. To understand more fully the perfect nature of your heavenly Father, read Psalms. They tell of His kindness, integrity, and faithfulness. Here are several psalms that are especially helpful in seeing our Father's loving nature. *Read through as many as you like.* As you read, note especially what the psalmist is saying about your heavenly Father's nature in your notebook. Then personalize the quality with a statement, such as "My Father is _____." After you have written the statement, pause and meditate

on what that aspect of His nature means to you
personally.

Psalm 3	Psalm 89
Psalm 23	Psalm 91
Psalm 27	Psalm 103
Psalm 34	Psalm 111
Psalm 63	Psalm 145

C. For a more extended study of your heavenly Father,
   begin a "My Father" notebook. As you read through
   the Scriptures, be especially observant of statements
   that tell how God thinks and feels about you. Write
   these in your notebook in such a way that their
   insights will apply to your own life.

2. At the beginning of this chapter, I asked you to imagine
   yourself in two situations where you needed the presence
   and strength of another. Think about actual past or
   present situations where your Father's presence, strength,
   and love would make a difference. Visualize Him present
   in those situations. Try to sense how His presence would
   give you new confidence, hope, and strength.

3. Memorize one of the following verses.
   "The LORD is gracious and compassionate, slow to anger
   and rich in love" (Ps. 145:8).
   "Let us approach the throne of grace with confidence, so
   that we may receive mercy and find grace to help us in
   our time of need" (Heb. 4:16).

Personal Feedback

1. Many of us have been taught to live independent, self-
   sufficient lives. Discuss together what the implications of

this are for problem solving. Ask others whether they see you as independent, dependent, or interdependent.

2. I quoted A. W. Tozer as saying that "the man who comes to a right belief about God is relieved of ten thousand temporal problems." Share specific examples where your confidence in God has relieved you of problems.

3. What people in the Bible, other than Joseph and Paul, solved problems effectively by relying on God's presence and strength? Discuss how their view of God made a difference in the outcome of specific situations.

4. Think of a problem or trial that you are currently facing. Share it, then answer the following questions with your group.
   A. What is your attitude toward the problem?
   B. Who is in control of the problem?
   C. Where is the Lord in relation to the problem?

Chapter Four

LEARNING WHEN HURTING ...
THROUGH HOLINESS

For five years I have spoken at an annual family camp on the West Coast. Each year Winnie and I anticipate renewing friendships with people who attended the previous years. As we prepared this summer for the weekend, our conversation included thoughts about a couple who have five daughters.

As people began to arrive on Friday night, I saw our friends' sister and brother-in-law. After warm greetings they informed me that our friends were unable to attend the camp but had sent a letter. The following excerpt is especially significant.

About two weeks ago my wife, Sue, gave birth to our sixth child, a boy. Our new son, Andrew James, is an exciting addition to our five daughters, whom you've met. And I don't mind telling you it's already been a real learning experience. Within minutes of his birth we were informed that he has Down's Syndrome. Needless to say, we've been through a lot in addition to the usual newborn adjustments.

The first week was especially hard, working through our emotions and adjusting. But we've since come to grips with our expectations and now accept our situation. We feel very good about our family unit and our new addition, accepting Andrew with his limitations. We still see him as a special gift, just in different wrapping. We look to the future with anticipation of all the things we'll learn because of this little guy. I'm sure he'll be a catalyst in drawing our family much closer over the years.

What is God attempting to accomplish in this family's life? What is He trying to achieve in your family? Mine? Does He have a purpose in the problems and trials we continuously encounter? Is there any meaning to it all?

WHAT GOD IS ACCOMPLISHING

The Scriptures clearly state that God is a pure, righteous, holy Person. He is complete in every way—the only being that is absolutely whole, absolutely without defilement. Furthermore, in His love for man He is committed to bring every child of God to this same perfect completion. His own declaration "Be holy, because I am holy" expresses His intent to do so.

The apostle Paul spoke of this in his letter to the Ephesian church. He described the supernatural gifts God gave to their leadership, so that they in turn might prepare the large church family to function as a spiritually healthy unit. Why? " . . . so that the body of Christ may be built up until we all reach unity in the faith and in the knowledge of the Son of God, and *become mature, attaining to the whole measure of the fullness of Christ.* Then we will *no longer be infants.*"[1]

Later in this same letter Paul stated that Jesus Christ lovingly relates to the church in such a way as to produce holy purity within it. His great goal is to call the church into radiance, beauty, wholeness, and maturity.[2] He anticipates an eternal relationship with a bride that shares His life, His beauty, His holiness, His glory. Although the fulfillment of this magnificent plan cannot be completed on earth, the beginning steps are being applied to every child of God.

Because our gracious Father is holy, He is calling us to holiness. Because Jesus Christ is holy, He is nurturing holiness in His future bride.

HOW DO TRIALS AND PROBLEMS ACHIEVE THIS?

God's primary strategy to achieve practical holiness involves problems, trials, and suffering. From God's perspective we have already been made holy through the death of Christ on the cross. Through the active ministry of the Spirit within us now, the daily reality of holiness is being worked out in our lives.

We should not be surprised that growth in spiritual wholeness occurs this way. It is a basic principle of life, which operates even in the natural world. An authority on motivation says, "Obstacles are your friends; you can't grow without them."[3] Another speaking in a practical vein remarks,

> So you've got a problem? That's good! Do you know of a single instance where any real achievement was made in your life, or in the life of any person in history, that was not due to a problem with which the individual was faced?[4]

Yes, obstacles, problems, and trials are essential ingredients in healthy growth. Should we expect they would be any less vital to spiritual life and maturity?

When the apostle James wrote to first-century Christians, he explored the crucial place of trials in spiritual development. They are so valuable, said James, that we should welcome them with joy.[5] He identified three ways trials are invaluable to nurture spiritual health. Other New Testament passages suggest two additional ways.

Before exploring these, I would like to define the word "problem," used in this chapter as a type of trial. Consider that all problems are trials, but not all trials are problems. And not all trials are problems to be solved; some are to be endured. But all problems are trials that promote growth.

Now let's identify five positive ways problems can aid our spiritual growth. First, *problems have the potential to build our faith.* When we encounter problems, we face things that are incomplete and in need of correction or solution. A large percentage of problems are uncomplicated, so we handle them easily in the course of a day's activities. A smaller percentage are problems with serious implications. Many of these involve decisions and consequences that will have a major impact on us, our families, or others around us. The results of these decisions can be for good or bad, for health or harm, for building up or tearing down.

Frankly, we all face problems that are too big for us. Often we do not have adequate wisdom; sometimes we have limited strength; other times we are without proper resources. Or we simply do not have enough time.

What do we do?

Problems have the potential to turn us to God. They challenge us to draw on His limitless wisdom, His unmatchable power, His overwhelming resources. They invite us to explore His reality. They call us to apply biblical principles, then we experientially discover spiritual reality. We learn firsthand that God is a real person. We discover how He handles problems that are unresolvable to us and how we can draw upon His spiritual resources.

Problems allow "hands-on" training in godliness.

What is the outcome from this approach? Faith is strengthened when we're discovering God at work experientially. Scriptural principles become relevant as we become aware of available spiritual resources and how to use them. A meaningful faith begins to grow.

The Gospels are vivid witnesses of the faith-building process. Read any one of them and notice that problem after problem arises. As the disciples handled these situations, they were challenged to view life from a new perspective. At times it seems as though they were saying, "Ah, I'm beginning to see how one lives in the kingdom of God. I haven't arrived, but I'm beginning to see the light." None became spiritual giants overnight, but changes did become apparent.

Our lives are essentially the same as the disciples'. The Spirit of God leads us from one problem to another, so we may discover how to apply faith in rearing children, in facing unjust people, in working at the office, in coping with a medical crisis, in resolving a marital dispute. On and on the process continues.

At its most basic level, problem solving is an exercise in spiritual development. By turning from our natural, humanistic responses to God's wisdom, presence, and power, we discover firsthand a new way of living. A new supernatural lifestyle begins to emerge; a godly life takes shape.

James introduced us to the second potential to be gained from trials and problems. He said, "The testing of your faith develops perseverance."[6] Problems are fruitful to *develop stability*—a natural consequence of faith building. As we discover new resources through union with Jesus Christ, we are strengthened because life becomes less of a stumbling, fumbling, groping-for-answers existence. Faith is a growing certainty about who God is and how to draw practically on His supplies.

It is helpful to notice how holiness, faith, and stability interrelate biblically. We can observe this in Paul's letter to the Colossians. The three words are brought together in chapter one, verses 22 and 23. In verse 22, Paul referred to the work of Christ in providing for our redemption and its practical results—our being presented before the Father as holy individuals. In verse 23, he identified the natural outworking here on earth—a growing faith developing stability in Christian living. The same interplay of dynamic faith and stability in lifestyle is described in Colossians 2:5–6 and 1 Peter 5:9.

Christians often express frustration at their lack of consistency in godliness. A close look usually reveals the root issue: weak faith. The believer does not have strong conviction in God's ability to act powerfully in difficult situations. Consequently, he takes matters into his own hands; this leads to failure, frustration, and instability. Although he may find a solution in his own strength, it is not a solution that builds confidence in the Lord. Many Christians experience these patterned responses, which are ultimately unsatisfying.

A third benefit can be gained through problems. James said that *problems have potential to bring wholeness* to our lives. As a person turns more and more often to God for strength and sufficiency, a higher level of confidence in Him is established. Our faith gains a firmness. The result is a healthy stability in coping with daily situations. As stability deepens, it provides this third benefit: spiritual health and wholeness. One writer summarizes the entire process in the following statement: "Trials test out for possible weak spots so as to make us genuine and solid all around."[7]

Spiritual wholeness is God's goal for each child of God. In our earthly lives we are challenged by parents and teachers to become mature. We all enjoy seeing an emotionally healthy individual. (How unfortunate that many life experiences defeat this rather than enhance it.) How much greater is our loving Father's desire to bring us to spiritual maturity and wholeness. James wisely observed that God gives us a variety of different trials ("of many kinds") to develop different areas of our lives. We face problems of many kinds to bring maturity to the entire spectrum of our personality. For example, God is not satisfied if we only have a clear mind but faulty emotions. Christ's radiant, pure, mature bride is to be lovely in every way.

A careful reading of Scripture indicates at least two other potential benefits from problems. Paul in his second letter to the Corinthians noted that the troubles and challenges we face have *the potential to produce empathy, which is a crucial element of love.*

Thank God, the Father of our Lord Jesus Christ, that He is our Father and the Source of all mercy and comfort. For He

gives us comfort in our trials so that we in turn may be able
to give the same sort of strong sympathy to others in theirs.
Indeed, experience shows that the more we share Christ's
suffering, the more we are able to give of His encouragement. This means that if we experience trouble, we can pass
on to you comfort and spiritual health; for if we ourselves
have been comforted, we know how to encourage you to
endure patiently the same sort of troubles that we ourselves
endured. [8]

Recently a lady shared with me a powerful example of
empathetic love. A family member who had alienated
himself from her for several years had experienced great
distress. He reached out to her for love and support. In her
own trials she had found God's power, growing stability,
and health, so she was able to be an unusual source of
strength to him. Her own struggles had equipped her to
enter into another's more completely.

Empathy is at the heart of all effective nurturing. We can
empathize because we, too, have faced enormous problems,
painful trials, or overwhelming challenges through which
we have discovered God's presence and strength. Now we
can extend loving support to others.

Problems have potential to exhibit God's glory and character.
This is expressed in two ways. First, God's presence and
help to us through our problems causes us to exalt Him in
worship and praise. As confidence in our Lord deepens, we
desire to honor Him. Second, others see a living faith
demonstrated through us. They recognize the presence of
the Holy One. They are challenged to praise Him because of
the faith, stability, and maturity they observe in us.

To summarize, problems produce holiness. Repeatedly I
have stressed the word "potential"—trials and problems
have the *potential* to work for good. If we ignore problems,
act foolishly, or allow unhealthy attitudes to dominate us,
the *potential* will be lost. I recall hearing a college professor
say that he had twenty years of teaching experience.

Someone later remarked, "Yes, but it was twenty years of bad experience!" Similarly, twenty years of ineffective problem solving is of little value.

HOW SHOULD I APPROACH PROBLEMS?

I have been saying to you that problems are invaluable assets to our growth. Don't ignore them! Approach each one as a growth opportunity. Keep an alert mind, then you can apply practical guidelines.

First, problems should call forth joy, not complaint. James counseled us to be joyful when problems come our way. Problems should prompt joy; they will *if* we honestly see them as growth opportunities. Our attitude is pivotal and will help avoid conflict and strife. A person who views problems positively, as opportunities to grow, will more likely use a constructive approach toward others. A person who views problems as a punishment, a threat to security, or an attack will more likely use a destructive conflict approach toward others.

To suggest that we not complain is not to deny the discomfort that problems can bring.

> The thought is that, when trials come, a lot of joy comes to people of faith. There is no denial that trials also produce strain and pain; there is, however, the reminder that, when they come, and when we evaluate them aright, we ought to bear them with joy. The flesh will not like them, but the spirit will rejoice to prove itself and to gain from the trials what Christ intended should be gained. [9]

The joy James spoke about is the joy of faith—joy that sees beyond the negative, painful problem to a higher purpose. We discover joy because we realize this is a new opportunity to experience the reality of God's kingdom life.

Second, we are to be careful about praying for escape or for easy solutions to problems, because we are actually requesting to remain immature, not to grow. As we pray about new challenges we are facing, we should be discerning about *how* to pray. Pray in a manner that is consistent with God's purpose. What does God want to produce in me?

Often the problems that are the most difficult to solve are the ones with the greatest potential to transform our lives. These require thoughtful, discerning prayer. Replace escapism prayer with prayer that will deepen your faith and invite God to form holiness more completely in you.

Pray with anticipation. Ask the Spirit of God to form an attitude of expectancy within you. Honestly look forward to some new positive outcome from the difficulty you are encountering.

Here's a final guideline for approaching problems: Practice a humble, inquisitive attitude. I find the following questions helpful. (1) What can I learn about myself through this experience? (2) Am I honest about facing this issue? [Am I blaming someone else? Am I blaming God? Am I skirting the real issue?] (3) What is God asking me to do? (4) What is God trying to teach me about Himself?

The premise of this chapter is that problems and trials are God's occasions to form practical holiness within us. One of His great longings is to make us like Himself, to transform us into the image of Jesus Christ. Therefore, we should treat problems seriously. Failure to do so cheats us of spiritual health and vitality and God of His glory.

Personal Discovery

1. Think of two significant problems you have experienced. Jot down the circumstances related to each. Then think through the following questions.
   A. How did they cause you to mature?
   B. How did your perception or attitude stimulate or hinder growth?
   C. How did you feel about them at the time?

D. Which problems, challenges, or trials have you faced with joy? What circumstances encouraged the spirit of joy?

2. Write down a problem, challenge, or trial that you are now facing. Think through the circumstances that relate to it. Then, answer the following questions.
   A. What attitude would you like to adopt toward current or future problems?
   B. What has this chapter suggested to enrich your thoughts and attitudes toward problems?

3. Reread the excerpt from the letter at the beginning of this chapter. Try to list five potentials family members can learn from this experience in the days ahead. One has already been suggested at the end of the letter. What personal qualities may Andrew help form in his family's members?

4. Scan through your newspaper. See how many news items you can find that tell of problems, tragedy, or trials. Try to think of what the people involved in these situations could learn if they viewed the situation from the perspective of James 1:2–4. Visualize yourself in these situations. How would you likely respond? How would you *like* to respond?

Personal Feedback

1. Make a list of all the major tasks and problems that a child must solve from birth to first grade to be a well-adjusted individual. After completing the list, discuss together the following questions.
   A. What would happen if a child refused to deal with a problem, such as learning to walk?

    B. What attitude do children most commonly have in relation to these growth experiences?

    C. How does the parent's perceptions of, and attitude toward, the child's growth tasks influence how the child copes with life?

    D. How is the maturity process of a child like the spiritual maturing of an adult?

2. Discuss what the following Scriptures teach us about problems and God's commitment to lead us to maturity.
    A. Psalm 107:4–8, 10–15, 17–21
    B. Psalm 119:71
    C. Luke 10:38–42
    D. Acts 16:22–34
    E. 1 Peter 1:6–7

3. Read the following quote by William Barclay. Talk over what encouragement or counsel he has for each of you concerning your attitude or concerning a specific problem you are facing.

All kinds of experiences will come to us. There will be the test of sorrows and the disappointments which seek to take our faith away. There will be the test of the seductions which seek to lure us from the right way. There will be the tests of the dangers, the sacrifices, the unpopularity which the Christian way must so often involve. But they are not meant to make us fall; they are meant to make us soar. They are not meant to defeat us; they are meant to be defeated. They are not meant to make us weaker; they are meant to make us stronger. Therefore we should not bemoan them; we should rejoice in them. The Christian is like an athlete. The heavier the course of training he undergoes, the more he is glad, because he knows that it is fitting him all the better for victorious effort. [10]

Chapter Five

PUTTING PEACE INTO PROBLEM SOLVING

I recall a leadership retreat where I asked church leaders to think of a word or phrase that described them as a team. One group of elders chose the phrase "Neurotic Intensity." They were men who were committed to Christ and His church, but they typically found themselves enmeshed in neurotic behavior when they worked as a team. Problems were magnified; solutions came with struggle.

Some of these men revealed personal turmoil. Inner peace was absent. Therefore, it was difficult to be at peace with each other when they were not at peace with themselves.

This story can be contrasted with an account from the life of the well-known missionary Hudson Taylor. One day he was standing on a riverbank in China, waiting for the boatman to come and transport him to the other shore. As the small craft moved toward the dock, a wealthy Chinese man bumped Hudson Taylor. He roughly shoved him aside; Taylor fell in the mud. Since the missionary was dressed in native garb, the wealthy man assumed he was a Chinese commoner, unworthy of respect.

Taylor got to his feet silently. The boatman, however, was angry. "I'll not take you in my boat," he said to the wealthy man. "This man was first; I take him." The wealthy traveler began to see his own selfish behavior. When Taylor invited him to join him in the boat, he was amazed at the lack of hostility in the man he had abused. The godly Mr. Taylor welcomed the opportunity to tell of God's gracious love.

These contrasting illustrations point out the significance of our inner state as we face stress, trials, and problems. Where anxiety, hostility, or bitterness reigns, problems degenerate into conflict. Where peace reigns, solutions come much more quickly. The peace of God is an indispensable resource to the child of God as he attempts to solve problems responsibly.

WHAT IS PEACE?

Shalom is an important word in the Hebrew language. Even today you may hear it spoken as a greeting, farewell, or blessing to the hearer. The root meaning speaks of "soundness," "completeness," or "well-being." Biblically speaking, it is more than psychological peace; it is a spiritual reality, rooted in the presence and activity of God.

The New Testament word for peace is *eirene*. "It is more typical of the NT . . . to relate the concept of peace to the notion of the salvation of the whole man."[1] Like the Old Testament's usage, "peace" expresses a spiritual reality: "The fruit of the Spirit is . . . peace."[2] This verse summarizes the New Testament's teaching. Fullness of peace cannot be experienced apart from the indwelling Lord.

The apostle Paul suggested that God-generated peace is a powerful, comprehensive reality. In 1 Thessalonians 5:23, he stated that God's personal peace should permeate our total being . . . spirit, soul, and body. In his subsequent letter, he enriched this truth by suggesting that "the Lord of peace himself give you peace *at all times* and *in every way*."[3]

What is peace? I believe that a summary of biblical teaching reveals that peace has three aspects: (1) a spiritual reality that comes through the presence of the God of peace; (2) a sense of well-being that permeates our entire person-hood; (3) a spiritual health that equips us to cope success-fully with the pressures of daily living.

PROVISIONS FOR PEACE

My research in the Word of God has produced a deeper appreciation for our loving Father's abundant provision for us. It seems apparent that He intends for us to experience a fullness of peace. His plan for us is to have health in spirit and mind, which allows us to face problems with clarity. So he provides a way for our lives to express an ongoing paradox: a life of complete peace in the midst of pressures, demands, and trials. To accomplish this He has made four provisions for our peace.

The first provision for peace is the *peace that comes through reconciliation*. God began His peace initiative by bringing us to peace with Himself. The Bible indicates that we were sinners, alienated from God. The death of Jesus Christ was the Father's means of dealing with this alienation from Himself. Paul stated concisely God's full provision for our reconciliation: "Therefore, since we have been justified through faith, we have peace with God through our Lord Jesus Christ, through whom we have gained access by faith into this grace in which we now stand."[4]

This provision has great practical significance: We can live without fear of alienation from God. We have confidence that our guilt before God has been removed permanently. Approaching Him, we can know the sin that separated us from Him has been removed by Jesus' sacrifice on our behalf.

Both Peter and Paul recognized that inherent in the "good news" of salvation was the good news of peace.[5] Imagine someone running through the streets of a city crying out, "Good news! Good news! God's wrath has been taken away. Peace has been established."

Even the Old Testament prophet Isaiah foresaw the impact of God's salvation and the Spirit's ministry bringing righteousness. Isaiah said, "the fruit of righteousness will be peace; the effect of righteousness will be quietness and confidence forever. My people will live in peaceful dwelling places."⁶ Peace with God leads to a quiet, restful spirit; it produces a confidence in our standing with God. Because we are at peace with Him, we have a basis for building peace with others and do not act out of unresolved guilt before God.

As meaningful as the peace of reconciliation is, it is only the beginning. Upon this foundation the Lord builds a second provision for personal peace—*peace that comes through relationship*.

Relational peace is possible because God by His very nature is a God of peace (Rom. 15:33, 16:20; 2 Cor. 13:11; Phil. 4:7; 1 Thess. 5:23; 2 Thess. 3:16). God cannot act at times peaceful; at other times, not. In His essence He is peace; He cannot be nonpeaceful. Thus, we are relating to a person of peace.

Relational peace is also possible because the God of peace establishes a personal relationship with us. He comes to live in union with us: Our lives in Him; His life in us (John 14:18–20, Col. 3:3–4).

Relational peace is possible for a third reason. A unique feature of God's sovereignty is that He can share His nature with His children. As He lives within us, His own life permeates our lives to the extent that His life flows into ours. His peace becomes our peace. Observe these verses:

"Peace I leave with you; my peace I give to you."⁷

"The fruit of the Spirit is . . . peace."⁸

"The peace of God . . . will guard your hearts."⁹

These are not sentimental statements but clear promises from the Lord. To those who will receive them by faith He gives His own peace. Our personal peace becomes inseparably linked to His presence within us. As we experience a reverential friendship with the Lord of peace, His peace spills into our lives, fostering a spirit of peace within us.

The writer of Hebrews pointed out that the presence of the God of peace within us equips us to do the will of God. It strengthens us to act in a positive manner, serving the Lord and ministering to others from a peaceful posture.

Another important result comes from having a relationship with the God of peace. As we relate to Him and His peace flows into our lives, we receive power and motivation to be at peace with each other. As Paul developed his message to the Ephesian church, he described God's redeeming love for mankind that led to our salvation.[10] Then he pointed out a second result of knowing the God of peace: Christ as our personal peace destroyed the wall that separates us from each other. The basis for our interpersonal hostility, resentment, and evil is removed. "For He Himself is our peace, who has made the two one [Jew and Gentile] and has destroyed the barrier, the dividing wall of hostility."[11] While the immediate reference in the passage was to Jew/Gentile hostilities, the implication is clear: God has made a way for Christians to be at peace with each other. The God of peace calls each of us to Himself, then unites us to each other. In His peace we find peace with each other.

The story is told about a tribe of fierce West African natives who held a mountain stronghold. Government troops had never succeeded in moving through this area. One day a missionary set out alone and traveled through the enemy land. The commander of the troops expressed amazement that he had not been harmed. The missionary replied, "You went as men of war; I went as a man of peace."

His statement is not abstract theology, idealism, or fantasy. We, as well as he, have a working basis to be people of peace—a unique, realistic basis to confront problems and difficulties without being anxious, angry, or fearful. God's living presence is to be our daily reality.

God's third provision is for *peace that comes through release*.

Our Lord does not make idle promises. Neither does he lead us to believe that we will escape problems, trials, and suffering. Jesus spoke in a straightforward manner to his

disciples. "In this world you will have trouble."[12] A careful
reading of the Book of Acts demonstrates clearly the
abundance of troubles they encountered; however, Christ
never intended his followers to be demoralized by trials and
opposition. Before he said, "In this world you will have
troubles," He said, "In me you may have peace. Take heart!
I have overcome the world."
Philippians 4:6–7 provides the basis for us to release our
anxieties and worries.

> Do not be anxious about anything, but in everything, by
> prayer and petition, with thanksgiving, present your requests
> to God. And the peace of God, which transcends all
> understanding, will guard your hearts and your minds in
> Christ Jesus.

Observe a three-step releasing process. *Step 1:* I decide or
choose not to worry or be anxious ("Do not be anxious
about anything."). No one makes me worry. I choose to
worry; therefore, I can choose not to worry. The Lord has
given us a healthier option, so we can choose. This leads us
to the next step.

Step 2: I bring my problem to God in a specific way. First,
I express thanks to the Lord, because I honestly believe that
God is sovereign and good. If He is sovereign, then He's in
control, which doesn't mean that He will solve the dilemma
the way I want it solved. If He is good, then I can have
confidence that He will act in a manner that is for my *ultimate*
good.

If I sincerely believe this, I have a valid basis, which is
rooted in my confidence in God, to release my anxiety. The
request is shaped by my genuine desire that God be honored,
by my confidence that He will guide me *through* the problem
situation, and by my commitment to let Him guide me *to* a
healthy solution.

All of this must be done honestly from the heart, and with
a sincere willingness to let God oversee the problem-solution

process. If we secretly plan to manipulate God or other people, we immediately nullify the possibility of seeing God's best solution. This is not to say that we do not apply ourselves to find a solution, but we do so only under God's leadership.

Step 3: I allow the peace of God, which will not necessarily follow logic, to guard my mind and emotions. At this point I have released the worry and anxiety by committing the problem to God's leadership. Therefore, I do not have to carry the responsibility for its outcome; I only have to act in response to His directions.

Observe that this releasing process calls forth my sensitivity to the Lord and His ways. It motivates me to study the Scriptures and see what He has said about His *modus operandi*. It challenges me to quietness, so I can hear Him when He speaks. It prompts growth.

God has yet another provision: *Peace comes through rule.* We are instructed in Colossians 3:15 to, "Let the peace of Christ rule in your hearts, since as members of one body you were called to peace." "Rule" in this verse implies umpiring. How are we to understand the peace of Christ acting as an umpire?

Note that Colossians 3:15 is recorded in the context of verses dealing with relationships among believers. The previous verses give guidelines for healthy relationships, energized with the spirit of love. Then in verse 15, Paul said that we are a Christian family, "members of one body." Christ's peace is to be the ruler, the decision maker, the umpire in our problem situations. We remove ruling from the "leaders" and give it to Christ who is Peace.

This is a crucial point: We give the authority of problem solving to Christ. He, the God of peace, rules. I give up my right to dictate the solution or to manipulate you. You do the same. Christ supervises the process.

This is a crucial point because it not only puts leadership in the correct place, it also tests our seriousness about a life of faith. Do we honestly believe that Jesus Christ will involve Himself in our problems? Do we dare trust Him? Does the Bible mean what it says? Or are these merely inspirational thoughts? We are challenged to release worries, anxieties, and rulership to Another. Few of us find this easy. We delight in hanging on to them and then complain about our situations. We are also challenged to live under the authority of the God of peace and take His Word seriously. The Word of God is incredibly relevant to our problems.

PEACE AND PROBLEM SOLVING

We have seen that our gracious Father has made abundant provisions for us to live in peace. He shares His own nature as peace and gives us a clear strategy to allow His active involvement in our problem situations. What practical effect can we expect, then, when He is present, and in charge of our problem solving?

God's indwelling peace gives us a spiritual-emotional health for problem solving. The mental and emotional rubbish that clutters our minds is removed. When anxiety, worry, and mental distraction occupy our minds, we are hindered from creative thinking and from constructive solutions. So we burn valuable energy wastefully. And we find it extremely difficult to hear the voice of God, or anyone else's.

Problem solving is enriched when the Lord leads it. His resources are made available to us; His quiet strength empowers us; His wisdom enriches our thought processes and helps us think clearly, productively, positively. Our minds are stabilized, so we can approach problems orderly and efficiently.

Few Christians seem to experience the level of peace in problem solving that I have described here. It takes courage to launch into a totally new way of responding to life's situations. This approach is radically different from what the majority of us have been taught all our lives. It is radical because it takes God and His ways seriously, because it centers on God's wisdom. We have been taught through a world system that does not take God and His wisdom seriously. Thus, the approach outlined in this chapter involves a new way of perceiving and acting.

This chapter also introduces an approach to problem solving that we *learn*. One cannot hear these principles and implement them quickly. They must be carefully digested, then we begin to practice them. We can anticipate the same success and failure we will have as we learn any new approach to life. However, the individual who faithfully follows the guidelines God has kindly given us will discover more and more success as the way of peace becomes familiar.

Personal Discovery

1. List any worries, anxieties or fears that rob you of peace. Beside each one write down a character quality God has that is able to deal with it. If possible, find Scripture that promises the availability of God for that need. Here's an example.

   A. Fear of the dark—God is always present to protect me (Ps. 27:1).

   B.

   C.

   D.

2. Review the three-step process that I described after God's third provision for peace. How can the process be applied to the situations you have identified above? Try to think through each one to understand what you can do to receive peace.

3. Write a letter to yourself explaining how one of the "peace stealers" in question 1 has affected your life and how, through God, you can be free from its destructive power. Read the letter daily as a reminder of your intent to look to God to deliver you.

4. Read through Matthew 6:25–34. Write down three principles that Jesus gives to help us find peace. Look over the principles and decide how consistently you practice them in your own life.

5. Memorize Philippians 4:6–7.

Personal Feedback

1. Share with another person a time when you were lacking peace and tell how it was established.

2. I have said that as the Lord lives within us, His Spirit of peace penetrates our lives. Discuss how consistently you have Christ's peace in your life.

3. If one of you lacks the peace of God described in this chapter, you might consider having a Bible study together to explore more fully what the Scripture says about His provision for peace in our lives. Begin by looking up the verses identified in this chapter.

Chapter Six

THE SECURITY OF HEAVEN FOR YOUR PROBLEMS

Burt and Pam* arrived at the renewal center—weary, discouraged, and defeated. The "ups" and "downs" of the past five years had taken their toll. At this point they were definitely "down."

As Burt poured out his story of pain and frustration, I detected recurring themes; one centered on Burt. In his desperate need for success, he compromised Christian convictions by accepting employment that led to painful relationships with co-workers. This pattern had occurred more than once. Now growing anxiety was gnawing at his subconscious: "I'm doomed to be a failure."

Pam was also hurting emotionally. Her mother's early years had been lived in poverty, so she vowed that her children would never know want. During her childhood and youth Pam heard again and again: "Give your children the best education possible. Don't make them the victims of poverty." Now Burt's job failures had brought the family dangerously close to poverty. As a result of debts mounting daily, disturbing thoughts plagued Pam: "I'm failing my children. They will never get to college. They are not well dressed. I'm ashamed that I'm not adequately caring for them."

Most of us recognize something of Burt and Pam within

*not their real names

us. Fear! Anxiety! Insecurity! Failure!—all seem destined to control our future because they can poison our good intentions and sabotage healthy relationships. Is there no freedom from such distressing feelings?

One biblical theme stands boldly against our sense of inadequacy. This recurring theme can give us great encouragement as we face distressing problems. Intended as a tower of strength, here's the theme.

God is powerful . . .
       sufficient . . .
       competent . . .
       able . . .
       willing . . .
       wise . . . to meet my legitimate need.

More than any other biblical principle, God's sufficiency challenges me repeatedly. He is committed to meet all my needs. Within His very nature, within His essence, He has complete resources to meet every genuine need I will ever have. Imagine the wonder of it: Every need you and I have should be met in *who God is*. The entire record of biblical history is a witness to this truth. The Lord has *never* failed to meet the legitimate need of one of His children when that person turned to Him in honest, complete trust.

FOUR PROVOCATIVE QUESTIONS

The apostle Paul expands on the theme of God's sufficiency in Romans 8 with a series of questions. These questions cover every situation that we will ever face. They are summary statements of the grand biblical theme: God is ready, willing, and able to meet every true need we face.

Question 1: "If God is for us, who can be against us?"[1] The obvious implication of the question is that no one can stand against God and His purposes. Therefore, if we believe that God has *guaranteed* our security, then we need fear no one. No matter what problem or trial we encounter, if God is in control, He will use it for good in our lives. The power behind this question is a power to liberate us from the fear of man or circumstances.

Question 2: "He who did not spare His own Son, but gave Him up for us all—how will He not also, along with Him, graciously give us all things?"[2] Again, the implication is clear. Our compassionate, gracious Father will make provision for every legitimate need we will ever face.

As David said, "The Lord is my shepherd, I shall not be in want."[3]

As Jesus Christ said later, "If you, then, though you are evil, know how to give good gifts to your children, how much more will your Father in heaven give good gifts to those who ask Him!"[4]

As Paul said, "My God will meet all your needs according to His glorious riches in Christ Jesus."[5]

The Lord doesn't promise to make us materially affluent; He doesn't promise to protect us from problems; He doesn't promise to keep us from suffering for righteous principles. *He promises to provide abundantly of His warm, compassionate love; He promises His spirit of peace; He promises His joy: He promises His security in every stressful, dangerous situation.*

Question 3: "Who will bring any charge against those whom God has chosen?"[6] His answer? "No one." Christians are absolutely safe in God's loving arms. Individuals may accuse, intimidate, and slander us before others, but the fact that we are secure in Jesus Christ gives us power to face trials and conflicts.

Can you see the practical application of this absolute security? He strengthens us against fearful circumstances on earth. Recall the "imagining" exercise at the beginning of chapter four. When the young child stood with his hand in his kind, loving father's hand, he had greater strength to face an otherwise fearful situation.

Question 4: "Who shall separate us from the love of

Christ?"⁷ The clear answer, "No one." We are always encircled by the personal, unconditional, compassionate love of Jesus Christ. The experiential reality of His loving presence provides overwhelming strength to cope with fear, anxiety, and condemnation. The child of God is eternally secure in the love of Jesus Christ.

Paul followed his final question with a decisive note of triumph: "In all these things we are more than conquerors through Him who loves us."⁸ How does this apply to our everyday circumstances? Problems are God's means to transform our lives, to give us "hands-on" experience in walking with Him. As a child of God begins to realize his Father's absolute sufficiency *and* absolute security, that person begins to lose fear of people, situations, and events. Furthermore, he discovers an eagerness to confront trials and problems because he anticipates his Father's active participation in and through them. He does not have to manipulate people, situations, and events because he is confident that his all-wise, all-adequate Father is more than able to supervise all aspects of his life.

No need to fear you;
no need to fight you;
no need to manipulate you . . .
since God's in charge.

FOUR ENLIGHTENING ILLUSTRATIONS

The Old Testament patriarch Abraham enriches our understanding of God's sufficiency. This godly man demonstrates the practical application we are seeking. I have selected four events from his life to illustrate incidents where he did or didn't trust the Lord's adequacy to meet his needs.

Illustration 1: Abraham, Sarah, and Pharaoh⁹

Abraham and his attractive wife, Sarah, journeyed to Egypt to escape famine in their homeland. As they entered this ungodly country, Abraham realized that he faced a *problem:* "What if Pharaoh wants Sarah for himself? He can't help being attracted to her beauty. He's liable to dispose of me to get Sarah for himself. What shall I do?"

Let's pause long enough to ask ourselves, "What's Abraham's *need?*" He fears for his life. Evidently, he needs the confidence that he is totally safe under God's protective care. He must believe that God cannot handle the situation adequately, so he feels forced to take matters into his own hands. "I'll resolve the dilemma by lying to Pharaoh. I'll say that Sarah is my sister." (If we are honest, we can see some of Abraham in ourselves.)

What is the *outcome?* Abraham's deceit caused Pharaoh and his family to experience physical pain from God. Abraham was forced out of Egypt with hard feelings on the part of Pharaoh. The problem deteriorates into conflict. Only God's kindness keeps a disaster from occurring.

Illustration 2: Abraham and Lot[10]

The second *problem* Abraham faced involves overpopulation. His and Lot's herdsmen began to argue over land rights to graze sheep. To complicate matters, other herdsmen were also in the vicinity, using valuable land. The problem was how to resolve the bickering and have adequate land for their needs?

As before, let's stop and ask, "What's Abraham's *real* need?" I would suggest that Abraham needs confidence that he is under God's care and blessing no matter what the outward circumstances (God had granted his covenantal blessing earlier in Gen. 12:1–3).

Abraham's response to the problem is recorded in verses 8–10. He acted in a gracious, conciliatory, open-ended manner; he was not defensive, possessive, or bossy. He appeared comfortable in letting Lot make the first land choice; he indicated no fear that he would lose out.

And the *outcome?* First, no conflict. Second, God affirmed His promise to be generous to Abraham. Abraham continued to prosper because he was under God's care, not because he outwitted Lot.

Illustration 3: Abraham, Sarah, and Hagar[11]
The *problem* involved Abraham and Sarah. They were childless. To complicate matters, they were past the age of childbearing. Sarah felt the cultural indictment of being childless—no doubt prompted by her feelings of inferiority among the other women.

Again we must ask the important question, "What is the *real* need?" I suggest both Abraham's and Sarah's fundamental need is to trust God's reliability. Earlier He had clearly promised Abraham a son (15:4). This couple needed to believe that God keeps His word; He is trustworthy. They also needed patience to wait for God to act.

The *outcome* is tragic. Sarah took matters into her own hands. She urged her husband to have a child through Hagar, Sarah's servant. The result was intense conflict. When Hagar bore the child Ishmael, the birth event led to resentment and bitterness in Sarah. She lashed out at Abraham; she abused Hagar and drove her and the child from the home. Long-term consequences followed when a bitter hatred resulted between Ishmael and Isaac and their descendants.

Illustration 4: Abraham and Isaac[12]
Abraham again faced a difficult problem. This problem involved God's instruction to Abraham to offer his son Isaac as a human sacrifice to Him. Isaac was Abraham's only son by Sarah, the answer to God's promise and someone Abraham loved dearly. From a human perspective, it didn't make sense.

What about Abraham's *need?* Once more he needed confidence in God. He had to trust that the Lord knows what He is doing when nothing seems to make sense. He needed an answer to the question we all ask when facing certain problems: "Is the sovereign Lord trustworthy? Will He keep His word? Is He reliable?"

And the *outcome?* The problem was solved because Abraham knew God was reliable. When faced with this crisis his faith did not fluctuate; rather this man of God was "fully persuaded that God had power to do what He had promised."[13]

The illustrations from Abraham's life may seem melodramatic, but the issue is not how dramatic they are. The point is that they are true experiences from a man who was learning how to find his every need met by the living God. You and I face our own life experiences that may be frightening, overpowering, tempting, or discouraging. Our responses have important consequences. Abraham represents you and me in our challenges, our problems, our conflicts. At their core Abraham's problems were much the same as ours; we face problems, have similar needs, and enjoy or suffer the same kinds of outcomes. Like Abraham, our problem-solving responses are rooted in our confidence in an all-sufficient Lord, or our lack of it.

WHAT CAN WE LEARN?

How can we apply what we have learned in this chapter? Each of us senses the relevance of the issue to our personal lives. Let's explore three implications.

We can see that the more we understand and experience God's adequacy, the better prepared we are to solve relationship problems. (By the way, notice that Abraham's four problems were relational.) We never do this perfectly, but it is a valuable goal to pursue.

"Understand" and "experience" are two separate processes. Many Christians agree factually that God is all-powerful, all-knowing, all-present. But in daily life there is little or no reality of these truths. Life goes on by human energy, human wisdom, human solutions. Little or no awareness of, or commitment to, spiritual reality exists. If God is going to be a real person involved in our life issues, He will have to bust through our predetermined patterns and habits of self-sufficiency. Unfortunately, God doesn't like to violate our lives. If we don't invite Him to become our Source, He won't force Himself on us.

Abraham is an inspiring example of the godly person learning to draw upon God's life, fullness, and power. Tragically, many find Abraham irrelevant to the twentieth century.

A second implication can be seen. Conflicts are more likely to be rooted in persons than problems. Behind the scenes of unresolved problems, persistent conflict is a subtle issue. Someone is seeking, grasping, manipulating, demanding something that is only indirectly related to the professed problem. For example, an individual may have an insatiable thirst to control others. He demands his own way when it is clearly destructive to himself and others.

Notice the third implication: Problems often blossom into conflicts because we want others to meet needs only God can meet. Directly, or indirectly we say, "You are responsible to make me . . .

> happy,
> secure,
> significant,
> popular,
> content,
> entertained . . .

when only God can fill the deep void from which these human cries come forth.

What do we say, then, to the issues this chapter has explored? Only the living God is adequate to meet the needs for security and significance we all experience. We need to heed the Word of the Lord that Jeremiah recorded. "My people have committed two sins: They have forsaken me, the spring of living water, and have dug their own cisterns, broken cisterns that cannot hold water."[14] When we face difficult problems, will we manufacture our own cisterns, try to dip water from others' cisterns, or turn to the Living Spring and find fullness to meet every inner need?

Personal Discovery

1. In your personal notebook make a chart by using the format suggested below. After completing it, think through your response to the questions that follow.
   A. Think carefully about seven important needs you have. List them on the chart.
   B. Beside each need write down the name of the person(s) you usually expect to meet that need.
   C. In column three (REALISTIC), indicate whether your expectation of the other person(s) has been realistic, *and* whether the person has actually met your need. Evaluate this in light of what this chapter has said.
   D. In column four jot down the emotion you experience when your need is not met by the person listed in column two.
   E. In light of what you have learned in this chapter, are you putting pressure on others to meet needs that only God can adequately meet? What would be a healthier course of action?

NEEDS	PERSON(S)	REALISTIC	EMOTIONS
1.			
2.			
3.			
4.			
5.			
6.			
7.			

2. Think through your own responses to Paul's four provocative questions in Romans 8. It is easy to give simple academic answers. Try to wrestle with them on a personal level. Ask yourself, "How do the circumstances of my life indicate I am answering them?"
   A. "If God is for us, who can be against us?"
   B. "He who did not spare His own Son, but gave him up for us all—how will He not also, along with Him, graciously give us all things?"
   C. "Who will bring any charge against those whom God has chosen?"
   D. "Who shall separate us from the love of Christ?"

3. Tony Walter says of the Old Testament perspective on life, "Things which we see as basic needs—food, health, life itself—were not seen as needs which people struggled to provide, but as blessings from a divine Creator. Rather than striving to meet our inborn lacks and needs, there is a vision in the Old Testament of a people and a land richly endowed by God. 'The Lord is my shepherd, I will not lack' (Ps. 23:1). Even when wandering in the wilderness, the very symbol of lack and need, God provided for the children of Israel so that they lacked nothing. Modern people in our so-called affluent society, brought up to strive to meet their own needs and lacks through economic or psychological effort, have great difficulty comprehending this old Hebrew concept of the original affluent society, given by God. God's gift seems to offend modern pride in human striving."[15]
   A. Do you view life more from the Old Testament view than from that of our modern society?
   B. Write down specific areas where you would have greater security if you took more literally "The Lord is my shepherd, I will not lack."

Personal Feedback

1. Discuss these questions.
    A. What happens in a relationship when one person expects the other to meet needs God should meet?
    B. In what situations are you seen as being unrealistic in what you expect from others?
    C. In what situations do you deny that God is sufficient for all your needs?

2. Decide on an area of personal growth that relates to this chapter. Agree to pray daily for each other in the coming weeks and keep each other posted on progress.

Chapter Seven

GETTING MOTIVATED TO SOLVE PROBLEMS

Michael Faraday, the inventor of the first electric motor, arranged a meeting with William Gladstone, the prime minister of England. He needed Gladstone's backing to promote his new invention. The simple device was set before the prime minister.

"What good is it?" he asked.

Faraday replied, "Someday you will be able to tax it."

Obviously he did not invent the electric motor to raise taxes. Yet he knew what would appeal to Gladstone. He sensed that the prime minister would express interest in what would benefit the country's economy. Faraday was an insightful motivator.

We are exploring the dynamics of effective problem solving. At this point we can raise the questions: "What motivates individuals to discover healthy solutions to their impasses?" and "What motivations underlie conflict?" The answers to these two questions moves us a step closer to effective problem-solving strategy.

MOTIVATION FOR CONFLICT

The apostle James posed an insightful question in his brief letter to the dispersed Jews. He asked, "What causes fights and quarrels among you?"[1] We can ask, "What is the root cause of conflict?" Or, "What motivates individuals when conflict results?"

James's answer is helpful. He said that fights, quarrels, and conflict are rooted in "desires that battle within you. You want something but don't get it." Frustrated because these consuming desires are not met, the Christian turns to destructive behaviors to force the issue. Conflict follows.

James also pointed out the fact that the individual has not approached God with his need. If it is a valid need, the starting point should be the Lord. Instead, our pattern too often is to exploit others to fill needs that only God can meet.

The authors of *The Manipulator and the Church* believe that manipulation is man's basic strategy to get what he wants. They describe man as "the creator and the perpetrator of a vast manipulative system."[2] Modern man uses this approach as his *modus operandi*, his basic attack to achieve his personal goals.

Four characteristics are evident in the manipulator. He is *deceptive*. "He uses tricks, techniques, and maneuvers because he cannot trust the other person's honesty of motivation."[3] How often have you observed in yourself or others the tendency to manipulate others through deceptive means to achieve the desired end? What message does this behavior send to the other person? What are we saying to ourselves when we use such tactics?

The manipulator is *unaware*. The energy and concentration required to achieve his own selfish goals leaves him powerless to perceive the needs of others. He is so busy devising strategies to assure his own victory, he has no motivation to consider other people's perspectives. He is unaware of their insights, their solutions, and their concerns.

A manipulator is *controlling*. Rather than approach problem solving as a team effort, the manipulator uses control methods. At times he uses his deceptiveness to lead people to believe that they are a part of the process. In truth, the manipulator knows from the beginning what he wants, so he controls people, resources, and strategy to get what is in his best interests. People exist to meet his needs; therefore, he is not afraid to use, or abuse others.

A manipulator is *cynical*. He is distrusting. Since he employs deception in his own relationships, he expects to find others doing it, too. He finds difficulty trusting himself or others. This cynical attitude destroys the healthy environment for positive solutions; it fosters conflict, quarrels, fights.

A few examples from the hundreds we experience easily demonstrate our manipulative bent. We want something; we manipulate others to get it.

I *want* a home cooked breakfast. I *convince* my wife that she should get up and prepare it for me.

My child wants to stay up to watch a late television program so *he sulks and pouts* to get his own way.

I *want* a new car so I *tell myself* the old one is falling apart and *ridicule* my spouse when he says we can't afford a new car.

Our credit card is almost to the credit limit, but I *want that* so I . . .

We began looking at the subject of motivation through the eyes of the apostle James, who reminded us of a self-centered bent in the heart of man towards selfishness. We look out for "No. 1" (ourselves, not God). We fight for our rights, our decisions, our best interests. Manipulation becomes a comfortable strategy for problem solving, and unless we discover a healthier motivation, we are doomed to conflict.

MOTIVATION UNDERLYING BIBLICAL PROBLEM SOLVING

The famous painter Renoir suffered painful effects from arthritis. Yet he continued to paint. One day fellow artist and close friend Henri Mattise was visiting in Renoir's home. It grieved him to see his beloved friend endure the agony of pain necessary to paint.

"My friend, why do you continue painting when you are in such agony?" asked Matisse.

Renoir replied, "The beauty remains; the pain passes."

Whenever I think upon this incident, I am struck with Renoir's deeper understanding of life. He symbolizes the numberless examples of individuals who have expended their lives for something more than pleasure. History provides person after person who witnesses to the power of an unselfish life.

The supreme witness is given by Jesus Christ. Both in His teaching and His example He provides the answer we seek. The Bible clearly describes the motivating power that is available to fill the Christian's life. By the power of God's indwelling love, we find a true basis by which to live. We receive not only the power by which to live, but also the motivation.

Consider these witnesses:

Jesus Christ: "Who being in very nature God, did not consider equality with God something to be grasped, but made Himself nothing."[4]

Paul: "I am torn between the two: I desire to depart and be with Christ, which is better by far; but it is more necessary for you that I remain in the body. Convinced of this, I know that I will remain, and I will continue with all of you for your progress and joy in the faith."[5]

Moses: "He chose to be mistreated along with the people of God rather than to enjoy the pleasures of sin for a short time. He regarded disgrace for the sake of Christ as of greater value than the treasures of Egypt."[6]

Love for God

Both Old Testament Jew and New Testament Christian were called to a sincere love for the Lord.[7] They were to seek His honor; they were to exalt Him at every occasion. All life was to be approached with a God-consciousness. Today we face the same challenge. The child of God, earnestly desiring to live out his devotion, lives to honor the Lord. He desires that his attitudes and actions be in the best interests of Jesus Christ. He is sensitive that his behavior in no way discredits God's holy character and holy purposes. Paul presented this truth to his Philippian readers when he challenged them to "do everything without complaining or arguing, so that you may become blameless and pure, children of God without fault in a crooked and depraved generation, in which you shine like stars in the universe."[8]

Genuine devotion to Jesus Christ and a yearning to see God's name honored creates a powerful motivation for the child of God. As he faces problems and trials, he is reluctant to accept a solution that is out of harmony with God's best interest. This is true even if the Christian stands to gain something personally. Although his emotional desires may cry out to be satisfied, in his spirit he is committed to honor the Lord he loves.

A vivid example of this is seen in the godly man David. He had come to the aid of King Saul and destroyed the Philistine giant, Goliath. Saul then took the young man into his army. In no time David established himself as a successful warrior. He rapidly became a hero with the Israelites. When the masses began to chant "Saul has slain his thousands, and David his tens of thousands," the insecure king feared for his throne. He told himself that he must destroy David to preserve his own life.

King Saul then began a campaign to kill David. David became an innocent fugitive, and his life turned into that of a hunted man. Again and again he would have been killed, but for God's protection. Finally the day came when the evil king was within David's grasp. Now David could annihilate the one who had hunted him so unmercifully. David's own men urged him to kill Saul. In essence they said, "Now's your chance. The Lord has put Saul in your hands. Destroy him!"

David saw things differently. He understood that Saul had been placed as king of Israel by God's design. David would do nothing to benefit himself at God's expense; he would not seek his own advantage to God's shame. David's love for Jehovah overpowered his desire to rid himself of a frustrating problem. He wanted God's honor more than his own comfort. If the problem were to be solved, it had to be solved in God's way, not by man's manipulation. David's high honor toward God led God to honor him before man.

It will not be different today. The child of God who is motivated to solve problems in a manner that honors the Lord God will be blessed by the Lord.

Love for Others

A second powerful motivation for problem solving is provided by Jesus Christ Himself. He says to his disciples, "A new commandment I give you: Love one another. As I have loved you, so you must love one another. By this all men will know that you are my disciples if you love one another." [9] When we are motivated to love others rather than manipulate them, we will be committed to a problem-solving approach that is unselfish, constructive, and considerate of others' needs. With this powerful basis of motivation undergirding our lives, we can put the needs of others above our own.

If I love you . . .
    will I bully you?
    will I take advantage of you?
    will I overpower you?
    will I exploit you?
    will I treat your insights rudely?
    will I be sarcastic?
        I think not!

The story is told of a Union soldier who was wounded during the Civil War. As the battle was ending, General Lee rode by. The enemy soldier, weak as he was, found energy to look at Lee and exclaim, "Hurrah for the Union!" When Lee dismounted and came to the wounded enemy, the soldier felt certain he was about to be killed. To his surprise, Lee came to him with compassion. The great general said, "My son, I hope you will soon be well." The Union soldier felt ashamed of his own behavior. He said, "If I live a thousand years, I shall never forget the expression of General Lee's face." The kindness of the enemy spoke so deeply to the vengeful soldier, he cried after Lee left.

We may not face situations as dramatic; however, the situations we face, common as they may be, can be handled with the same compassion, courtesy, and respect that was shown on the battlefield. Many simple problem situations evolve into battlefields, where people are wounded without blood showing. Our challenge is to respond to the appeal of the apostle Paul as he urged believers to "make my joy complete by being like-minded, having the same love, being one in spirit and purpose. Do nothing out of selfish ambition or vain conceit, but in humility consider others better than yourselves."[10] I cannot help but believe that if this brought joy to the heart of Paul, it will bring an equal response to the heart of our Lord.

As we consider the thrust of this chapter, we are left with an important question related to our problem–solving approach. Will our motivation for problem solving be to gain what is best for ourselves, whatever that may cost others or the Lord? Or will our strategy be to adopt a problem–solving approach that incarnates Christ's words?

> " 'Love the Lord your God with all your heart and with all your soul and with all your mind.' This is the first and greatest commandment. And the second is like it: 'Love your neighbor as yourself.' All the Law and the Prophets hang on these two commandments."[11]

Personal Discovery

1. This chapter has focused on what motivates us to solve problems or enter into conflict. Below are a number of relationships a person may have. Beside each one jot down a brief description of a problem or conflict situation you have faced.

RELATIONSHIP	NATURE OF PROBLEM/CONFLICT
Father	_____
Mother	_____
Brother	_____
Sister	_____
Son/Daughter	_____
Work associate	_____
Teacher	_____
Schoolmate	_____
Neighbor	_____

   A. What motivated you to solve the problem in a healthy manner. What motivations existed that could have led to conflict?
   B. What motivations were apparent in the other person?

2. Think through the list of relationships above and choose one relationship in which you are *presently* facing a problem or conflict. What is motivating you or the other person to solve the problem in a healthy manner? What forces are tempting you to resist solving the problem in a constructive manner? Where are you using manipulation

to get your own way? Try to be honest in examining the underlying motivations at work within yourself.

3. Write a letter to God telling Him of your desire to solve the problem you've described above for His honor and for the well-being of others. Include what personal changes you are willing to make in your attitude or actions so that a healthy solution can result.
4. Examine the following Scriptures. Write down the problem as you understand it. Then, try to identify the underlying motivation that directed the individual. Finally, decide whether the person's motivation led to God's glory, others' well-being, or the individual's personal interest. Was the final result healthy problem solving or conflict?
   Genesis 3:1–7
   Genesis 45:1–11
   I Kings 12:1–11
   Acts 5:1–11
   Philippians 1:12–14

Personal Feedback

1. Read each of the following situations. Then discuss the possible positive and negative motivations that could be at work.
   A. A new employee has been hired. You are not fond of this woman because she gossips, distracts you from your work, and constantly complains about her marital problems. You are a close friend of your employer, and he respects your opinion. Is now the time to tell your employer what you think of the new employee?
   B. It is Friday afternoon, and your boss has told you that you are being given a considerable raise. You

think, "Wow, I can buy the new car I've wanted!"
But almost immediately a second thought arises:
"I've been praying for a way to help the needy. Is
this an answer to my prayer?"

C. A non-Christian friend calls and asks you to go
skiing next weekend, all expenses paid. You excit-
edly agree to go. After you hang up the phone, you
remember that you promised to teach Sunday school
next Sunday.

2. Discuss the following questions as they apply to your
lives.
A. Should a Christian always put himself last?
B. What are guidelines for meeting our own needs and
yet not neglecting the needs of others?

Chapter Eight

THE WORLD'S GREATEST POWER FOR A PROBLEM SOLVER

Problem solving is a demanding, humbling task. Ask any conscientious government leader. He can explain the incredible weight of responsibility a person feels when he accepts the call of leadership.

Let's examine the situation that faced Solomon as the king of Israel.

He was appointed king of Israel. [1] He followed in the footsteps of his father, David, who was an outstanding leader. After David had brought the nation to international prominence and extended its borders vastly, he passed the reins of leadership to Solomon.

Solomon was no fool. He understood his own feelings of inadequacy. The awesome task before him overwhelmed him. Thus, he left for Gibeon to set aside time for worship and dedication to the Lord. God seemed to know what was weighing on the young king's mind. He appeared to Solomon in a dream and said, "Ask for whatever you want me to give you." [2]

Solomon's response was telling. He unburdened his heart to the Lord with these words.

"Now, O LORD my God, you have made your servant king in place of my father David. But I am only a little child and do not know how to carry out my duties. Your servant is here among the people you have chosen, a great people, too numerous to count or number. So give your servant a discerning heart to govern your people and to distinguish between right and wrong. For who is able to govern this great people of yours?"[3]

Can you feel the impact of what Solomon said, of what he requested? He was not literally a "little child," but he *felt* that inadequate. When he pondered what was expected of him as a national leader, he *felt* unprepared to cope successfully with the situations he knew he would face. No doubt he had watched his father over the years as he faced difficult problems and observed the consequences of the decisions David had made. Now those kinds of problems were his; people expected him to be competent. But Solomon didn't *feel* competent! Thus, we can see that his request to the Lord was not made thoughtlessly. Solomon wanted help.

God is delighted when we turn to Him in our sense of inadequacy. The Bible says, "The Lord was pleased that Solomon had asked for this."[4] But we observe something even more significant: God responded to Solomon's request with a specific answer—a *new power* for problem solving. In essence the young king had asked for wisdom to enable him to make sound, helpful decisions; God equipped the king with a supernatural power unknown to man in that day.

Solomon returned home from his profound experience of God's enabling. Immediately his new power was called upon. He was faced with a baffling problem between two women. They stood before him with an infant, whom each claimed as her own. Solomon had to make a just decision. His God-given discernment enabled him to put a simple test before the ladies that revealed the true mother. His new-found power for problem solving worked.

Solomon's primary fame centered on this central truth: He asked for the power of wisdom and it was granted. He ruled in power because he ruled in wisdom.

A GOD OF WISDOM

A careful study of the Bible reveals that God is a God of wisdom. The following verses state this truth concisely.

"To God belong wisdom and power; counsel and understanding are his."[5]

"How many are your works, O LORD! In wisdom you made them all."[6]

"Christ the power of God and the wisdom of God."[7]

"Praise and glory and wisdom and thanks and honor and power and strength be to our God for ever and ever."[8]

The biblical perspective demonstrates that wisdom is basic to the essence of who God is. Being fundamental to His nature, wisdom finds expression in all His activities. He cannot act without wisdom because apart from God wisdom does not exist.

The wisdom of God is not merely superior knowledge. Since it is related to His being, wisdom reflects a total way of life. God not only *knows* but *is*, so His wisdom is demonstrated in every action He undertakes, as well as in what He knows or says. This is a powerful encouragement for the child of God, for it teaches us that all of God's activities toward us are undertaken with His nature of wisdom. Each event He plans for us is formed in wisdom and designed to accomplish some positive end, even if we cannot perceive it.

NEW POWER FOR LIVING

It's comforting for us to know that God's wisdom permeates His every act; however, an even more amazing fact emerges from our examination of His Word. *God wants to share His wisdom with His people,* according to the godly prophet Daniel. He had personally experienced a supernatural revelation from God. In answer to earnest prayer by Daniel and his friends, God had revealed the dream of King Nebuchadnezzar to him. Daniel's response to this outpouring of God's wisdom was expressed in his prayer of worship and adoration.

"Praise be to the name of God for ever and ever; wisdom and power are his. He changes times and seasons; he sets up kings and deposes them. He gives wisdom to the wise and knowledge to the discerning. He reveals deep and hidden things; he knows what lies in darkness, and light dwells with him. I thank and praise you, O God of my fathers: You have given me wisdom and power."[9]

Daniel confessed that wisdom comes from the Lord. Then twice in his prayer he acknowledged that God imparts that wisdom to His children. By giving His wisdom to Daniel, God equipped the young man to stand before the king and reveal insights that the king knew could only come from the Lord. In fact, Nebuchadnezzar was quick to recognize the source of Daniel's wisdom. He declared, "Surely your God is the God of gods and the Lord of kings and a revealer of mysteries, for you were able to reveal this mystery."[10]

I can imagine a reader saying, "Daniel is a special person. He was called to be a prophet. God revealed His wisdom to him because he had such an important mission in life. I'm just an 'average' person with no great mission. It's hard to believe that this powerful wisdom is available to me in the issues I face."

The good news is that the Lord wants to impart His wisdom and understanding to all who confess Him as Lord. Daniel didn't say that God gave wisdom only to him. Other biblical witnesses have proclaimed the same message: God delights to make His supernatural wisdom available to us as we confront problems. He doesn't want us to fumble and stumble through life; that brings no honor or credit to Him. Rather His intention is that as His people live in union and communion with His indwelling Spirit, His supernatural wisdom will guide and direct their lives. The more powerfully this operates within their lives, the more profound will their lives radiate His presence to an unwise and ungodly world.

I noted earlier that the wisdom of God is not merely

superior knowledge. More than knowing, it is being. Even so, being wise from a biblical point of view is a lifestyle for the child of God. Because it is a lifestyle, certain characteristics will emerge that we can see.

Godly wisdom is characterized by a *renewed mind*. In his letter to the Ephesian Christians, Paul exhorted them to "put off your old self, which is being corrupted by its deceitful desires; *to be made new in the attitude of your minds;* and to put on the new self, created to be like God in true righteousness and holiness."[11] In the midst of his challenge to godly living, Paul called for the emergence of a new way of thinking, influenced by the life of Christ penetrating our lives. "Renewing of our mind" suggests that wisdom is as much a new way of thinking as it is thinking new thoughts.

Few Christians realize how deeply our thought patterns have been formed by the world system in which we were reared. The majority of us attended schools that taught from a humanistic point of view, so we learned to view life from an individualistic, competitive perspective. We were taught to major in the "here and now," emphasizing the "scientific method," which only accepts what is observable, and to minor in the "spiritual" dimension of life, either by discrediting it, or by ignoring it.

Do you see that God's imparted wisdom must affect the thought process as much as the thought content? God is committed to renew our way of thinking as the foundation for wisdom.

Godly wisdom is characterized by *humility*. Many years ago when I was a young Christian, someone showed me Proverbs 3:5 as a foundational concept for my Christian life. "Trust in the Lord with all your heart and lean not on your own understanding." I questioned, "If God has given us minds, why not use them?" Over the years I've seen how limited my own understanding has been. So often I've made decisions without seeing the full picture. I've advocated a "biblical" point of view, only to realize later that it was traditional, or cultural, but not biblical. More and more I've learned to appreciate the wonder of my brain but have accepted with humility the unreliability of my mind to be absolutely discerning.

The famous inventor Samuel Morse was once asked if he ever came to situations where he didn't know what to do. Morse responded, "More than once and whenever I could not see my way clearly, I knelt down and prayed to God for light and understanding." He received many honors from his invention of the telegraph but felt undeserving. Said Morse, "I had made a valuable application of electricity, not because I was superior to other men, but solely because God, who meant it for mankind, must reveal it to someone, and was pleased to reveal it to me."

The apostle James described another characteristic of godly wisdom. He observed that "the wisdom that comes from heaven is first of all pure; then peace loving, considerate, submissive, full of mercy and good fruit, impartial and sincere."[12] The majority of the words he used to describe spiritual wisdom describe the way we relate to others. Godly wisdom—this wisdom God imparts to His seeking children—is *loving* toward others. James's description underscores the importance of how we relate to others as basic to true wisdom. We cannot justify arrogance, sarcasm, or selfishness in our lives and be persons of wisdom. People may say, "He sure knows a lot; he's a walking encyclopedia." But, we won't be "wise" in the biblical sense of the word.

A. W. Tozer noted,

. . . in the Holy Scriptures wisdom, when used of God and good men, always carries a strong moral connotation. It is conceived as being pure, loving, and good. Wisdom that is mere shrewdness is often attributed to evil men, but such wisdom is treacherous and false. These two kinds of wisdom are in perpetual conflict.[13]

A final characteristic of spiritual wisdom is its *power*. The writer of Ecclesiastes reminded us that "wisdom makes one wise man more powerful than ten rulers in a city."[14] The basic premise of this chapter is that God's presence within us equips us with a power to undertake problem solving—the power of wisdom. Godly wisdom gives us

> power to think as God thinks,
> power to see as God sees,
> power to be loving to others,
> power to harness our unhealthy desires,
> power to see the unseen.

RECEIVING GOD'S WISDOM

How do we receive God's wisdom? How do we tap into this power for problem solving? These questions lead us to the next step in our exploration.

We must recognize first of all that God's wisdom cannot be separated from God Himself. If His wisdom is part of His being, then we cannot have one without the other. To participate in God's wisdom requires us to come into relationship with God through His Spirit. The danger is that we accept this on an intellectual level, but not on the experiential level; we may agree with the concept, yet ignore it in actual application. Our tendency is to want God's wisdom, but not God's direction. God will have no part of this type of relationship. Either we will fully recognize who He is and what His claim is on our lives, or we will have to search somewhere else for His resources.

The wisdom of God is available to the believer through the Spirit of God. Since each Christian is indwelt by the Holy Spirit, he has the resources for wisdom within. In Paul's first letter to the Corinthians, he instructed them concerning the Spirit and His provisions for holy living. Paul said,

"No eye has seen, no ear has heard, no mind has conceived what God has prepared for those who love Him." But God has revealed it to us by his Spirit.

The Spirit searches all things, even the deep things of God. For who among men knows the thoughts of a man except the man's spirit within him? In the same way no one knows the thoughts of God except the Spirit of God. We have not received the spirit of the world but the Spirit who is from God, that we may understand what God has freely given us. [15]

Notice what Paul emphasized. First, God reveals his insights through His Spirit. Then, that one purpose for the Spirit living within the Christian is "that we may understand what God has freely given us." Last, the Spirit teaches us spiritual truths. This suggests the importance of a meaningful relationship between the child of God and the Spirit. Too often Christians tend to think that something "mystical" happens whereby the Spirit fills our minds without any relationship or participation on our part.

The Old Testament prophet Jeremiah identified an issue that disturbed the Lord. Jeremiah said that he had spoken the Word of the Lord again and again for twenty-three years "but you have not listened." Four times he emphasized "you have not listened."[16] Jeremiah told us of a common problem we all face: God can be speaking to us, endeavoring to reveal His wisdom, but we ignore His promptings for relationship and turn away to our own interests.

Our first challenge is to decide whether we want to receive God's wisdom badly enough to build a serious relationship with the Lord through His Spirit. The Scriptures clearly indicate that the Holy Spirit teaches us God's wisdom. Any teacher must have the student's time and interest, or little learning will take place.

Someone might argue that the Spirit only wants to teach us truths related to prophetic events, or high and lofty truths about God. While these are obviously within the scope of God's concern, a careful reading of the Bible makes it clear that God is equally interested in giving us wisdom concerning how to deal with human relationships and how to face life's many and varied problems. God's wisdom has a dimension that fits the practical demands of life.

A second clue to receiving God's wisdom is found in two biblical accounts already examined in this chapter. When Solomon recognized his need for supernatural wisdom, he *prayed* and asked for it. God answered the prayer in abundance. The same testimony was given by Daniel. Daniel affirmed, "You have made known to me what we asked of you."[17]

Serious prayer becomes a means whereby we can cultivate the relationship with God that leads to wisdom. As we begin to know Him, we begin to be filled with the wisdom that is part of His nature. He counsels us in His ways and guides us in His truth.

A third means that God uses to lead us into wisdom is His Word, the Scriptures. Paul said to the Colossians that they should "let the word of Christ dwell in you richly as you teach and admonish one another with all wisdom."[18] He identified the internalization of the Word of God as basic to wisdom—a principle that is repeated throughout the Scriptures. God reveals His wisdom through His Word.

Obviously, we need to be students of the Scriptures. It is especially helpful to read with a desire to discover principles that the Lord has demonstrated throughout biblical history to guide us in confronting life problems. The wisdom of the Scriptures has an eternal reality that provides insight for any age, any culture.

WISDOM AND PROBLEM SOLVING

In this chapter we have explored the power available for problem solving we can receive through God's wisdom. To close, we can see several implications directly related to problem solving.

First, we need to ask, "What is my attitude toward problems?" When I face them, do I quickly look to God for wisdom and insight? Do I recognize the limitations and dangers of solutions that I have been taught by others? Do I test out ideas and proposals with the Scriptures?

Second, we need to ask, "What is my attitude toward people who encounter problems with me?" Do I adopt a spirit of humility? Am I willing, even eager, to learn from them? Do I believe that the Spirit of God can reveal His wisdom through them? Do I have the wisdom to see inner issues, "hidden agendas," or other matters perceived through wisdom?

Third, we need to ask, "What is my attitude toward ungodly strategies that are sometimes considered wise?" Do I recognize that intimidating others, lording things over them, are foolish approaches to problem solving, even though others advocate them as ways to "get the job done?" Am I aware of my tendency to want to seek selfish interests?

These questions may help us consider the relevance of God's wisdom for our lives as we grow more competent and godly in facing problems. We do have a POWER that God has made available to us.

Personal Discovery

1. Proverbs is a book of wisdom. By reading a chapter daily, you can complete it in a month. Each day see what answers you can find to the following questions. Be sure to record your observations in your notebook. You'll find it valuable to look back over your discoveries.
   A. What is wisdom?
   B. What are the characteristics of a wise person?
   C. How does a person gain wisdom?

D. How does wisdom benefit a person?

2. What are the implications of the following statement to problem solving?

Wisdom, among other things, is the ability to devise perfect ends and to achieve those ends by the most perfect means. It sees the end from the beginning, so there can be no need to guess or conjecture. Wisdom sees everything in focus, each in proper relation to all, and is thus able to work toward predestined goals with flawless precision. [19]

3. In the section of this chapter entitled "Wisdom and Problem Solving," I raised a number of questions. Prayerfully work through these questions, applying them to your own life. Write down specific growth areas you want to work on related to this chapter.

Personal Feedback

1. What is our society's attitude toward wisdom? Are we more knowledge-oriented or wisdom-oriented? How does this influence us as Christians?

2. In 1 Corinthians 2, the apostle Paul distinguished between human wisdom and a wisdom that comes distinctly from God. Discuss together how the Christian relates to these two dimensions of wisdom.

3. In what way is wisdom power? Talk over your personal plan to gain "wisdom power."

4. Share specific problems you are facing in which you need godly wisdom. Agree to pray for each other in relation to these.

Chapter Nine

LOVE, RELATIONSHIPS, AND PROBLEMS

Allyson had never lacked boldness. So her mom and dad were not surprised when she approached them with a request.

"I'm old enough to be out on my own," she began. "It's time I had a chance to experience life for myself, without you two looking over my shoulder."

"Well, what do you have in mind?" her dad asked hesitantly.

"You two are well off financially," said Allyson. "I want you to give me money to move to Atlanta and live by myself. I need enough to rent a fashionable apartment, buy a new car, and have living expenses. I think I'd like to attend an art school for at least a year."

Neither parent was excited about the idea. Allyson liked having a good time and had never shown much seriousness about life. Yet, perhaps she needed this experience to establish herself as an adult. After all, she was nineteen. Her parents genuinely loved her and didn't want to dominate her life.

Allyson got the money; Atlanta certainly was an exciting place to live. Soon she had made friends who knew where all the "activity" was. Allyson decided that school could wait. "Why not have some fun while I'm young?" she reasoned to herself. She had plenty of money, and her newly found friends introduced her to lots of new places, new experiences, and new emotions.

The truth is, it was more than this nineteen–year–old could handle. What started out as "fun" became addicting. Before she realized what was happening, she was hooked on drinking, wild parties, and late nights. Three months later, Allyson realized she only had a hundred dollars left. The most devastating blow came when she found out that she was pregnant!

She didn't want to call her parents. So she began looking for a job. Because she was unskilled, all she could find was work that paid minimum wage. She tried keeping up with the bills that had accumulated during the "fun" time, yet she kept sinking deeper and deeper in debt. The truth hit her the night she began to cry uncontrollably with shame, fear, and loneliness.

"The only place I can go is home," Allyson said to herself. "But will Mom and Dad take me back? I'll be a disgrace to them. Here I am four months pregnant. I look like a bloated beggar."

I want you to pause in your reading for a moment and answer these two questions related to the incident described above.

If you were Allyson's parent, would you take her back into your home?
If you did, what would be the conditions?

Now consider a second account, paraphrased from the gospel of Luke.

A young man came to his father and asked him for his share of the family estate. The father gave his son his portion. After he gathered his possessions together, the son moved to a town some distance away and spent his fortune in "wine, women, and song." At about the same time, that part of the country experienced an economic depression, and the young man could not get a respectable job. Finally he secured work slopping the pigs. "Your pay is your food— the same as the pigs eat," said the farmer.

One day the young man came to a startling realization. "My dad's hired men have conditions far better than I do. I'm going to go home, tell dad how unworthy I am, and ask him to hire me on as a servant." So he set off toward home.

Unknown to the son, his dad had been looking for him for many days. When he saw his son coming down the road, his heart filled with overpowering emotion and his eyes welled up with tears. He ran down the road, threw his arms around his son, and kissed him. As they walked back down the road to home, the son shared his shame and asked for forgiveness. His dad heard it but was more concerned to express his delight at the son's return. He told the servant to get the best robe for his son. He gave him a family ring and sandals for his feet. Then he planned a feast to celebrate the return of his son.[1]

I'd like to ask you to pause again and make a comparison.

Compare your response to the first account with the father's response in this second account. How are they alike? How different?

PRIORITY ON RELATIONSHIP

Effective problem solvers know which issues are of crucial importance. These important issues then take higher priority in their planning and implementation. Ineffective problem solvers blunder along, following hunches, feelings, and opinions without any definite strategy that is consistent with a biblical theology. So often the results are disastrous.

Probably most people set some sort of priority in facing problems, but usually priorities are not thought through completely. For example, some individuals rely on *assigned position* to resolve problem situations. Consider these statements.

"You'll do what I say because I'm your *dad!*"

"My decision is more important because I was appointed as the Sunday school superintendent."

"I'm boss and what I say goes!"
"Since I'm your husband, what I decide is more important."
Others believe that they have more authority in the
decision because they are the *expert.* "I was trained in this
field and know far more than you ever will. Therefore I am
the only one capable to make a decision." Another person
relies on his *age,* or *length of service,* to hold social power over
others. "Sonny, when you get to be my age, you'll learn not
to make such dumb suggestions. Why don't you sit quietly
and listen to a wiser man."
We are much more effective in problem solving if we
place high priority on building and maintaining positive,
loving relationships with those people we live with, work
with, worship with, fellowship with. I often counsel parents
to approach problem situations with their children on a
relational basis, rather than a power basis. Having been a
parent for twenty-one years, I have consistently tried to
approach problems with my children on a relational basis,
rather than trying to emphasize my *position* as their dad or to
get into a power struggle with them. The results of this
approach have been very gratifying; I recommend it highly.
I am not saying that those placed in leadership positions
never need to call upon their authority as assigned leaders. I
am saying that it is unwise to *begin* by asserting authority.
We begin by asserting our love. Only when an individual
expresses open rebellion are we to resort to the authority of
the God-given position. Even then, we act in love.

POWER FOR LOVING RELATIONSHIPS

Problems are solved more effectively when loving relationships are cultivated. But where do we find the power to
love others when we face individuals who share different
opinions, different values, different motivations, different
lifestyles? Some individuals are hateful, obnoxious, manipu-

lative, unreliable, and argumentative. Where do we find
enough love to work with people like this? Look at the
diagram below.

GOD OF LOVE
AND COMPASSION

By now the answer should be obvious. I have been saying
that in Jesus Christ we find the resources to cope successfully
with problems. As with the earlier resources we have
investigated, God's love cannot be received apart from
receiving His very life. The Scriptures remind us that the
"fruit of the Spirit is love."[2]

Even a rapid scanning of the Bible will introduce the
reader to the overpowering theme of God's love for
mankind. His love is not expressed in a detached, impersonal
manner; He loves each individual He encounters intimately,
powerfully, eternally. Love is integral to who the Lord *is*,
not something that is passed on apart from His own
personhood. John Powell, in his book *Why Am I Afraid to
Love?*, expresses this concisely.

> More than this, God does not simply *have* love; he *is* love. If
> *giving* and *sharing* with another is the character and essence of
> love, then God is love. He can acquire nothing because he is
> God. He needs nothing because he is God. He has all
> goodness and all riches within himself. But goodness is self-
> diffusive; it seeks to share itself. So the infinite goodness
> which is God seeks to communicate, to diffuse, to share itself
> . . . with you . . . with me . . . with all of us.[3]

Probably the clearest, most powerful, well-known testimony of God's love for us is stated in John 3:16. "For God so loved the world that he gave his one and only Son that whoever believes in him shall not perish but have eternal life." It is but one among hundreds of verses in the Word of God that proclaim this truth.

God's love is a relational love, personal and intimate to each individual. The psalmist exclaimed, "the Lord is gracious and compassionate, slow to anger and rich in love."[4] These adjectives describe how one individual treats another in personal encounters.

The Lord is a gracious individual.
The Lord is a compassionate person; He has feelings toward me.
The Lord does not quickly lose His temper; He is patient with my imperfection.
The Lord has abundance of love for me.

These truths can be summarized in the second diagram on page 101.

In John Powell's quotation, he says that the nature of God's love is to be giving and sharing of Himself. God comes to share life with the believer, and in doing so His nature of love is planted within us. As we are united with the very life of Christ, God's love begins to penetrate our beings, just as heat from a stove radiates throughout a room to warm everything. God's spirit of compassion effects a change in our natures. We become loving because He is within us.

Many Christians and non-Christians have never experienced consistent, warm, intimate love from another person. As children, their lives were formed by cold, distant, busy, unaffectionate parents. As adults, they find it difficult to love others because they themselves have never known this compassionate, affectionate, self-giving love. Unfortunately, coming to personal faith in Jesus Christ does not automatically make it easy to love others. Vast numbers of earnest Christians know intellectually that God loves them, but they have never experienced that love in a personal, intimate, transforming way from another person. The loving Father, the loving Son, the loving Spirit indwell them; however, the *relationship of love* has never had a chance to blossom.

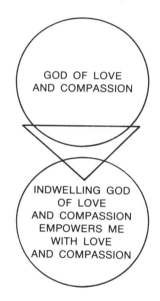

GOD OF LOVE
AND COMPASSION

INDWELLING GOD
OF LOVE
AND COMPASSION
EMPOWERS ME
WITH LOVE
AND COMPASSION

Most of us are not deeply aware of his fatherly, even tender, love. It is especially the person who has never experienced a human love, with all of its life-giving effects, who has never been introduced to the God who is love through the sacrament of human love, that stands at a serious disadvantage. The God of love, who wishes to share his life and joy, will probably seem like the product of an overheated imagination—unreal. [5]

When God's love penetrates us, that genuine love gets passed on to others, as the following diagram shows.

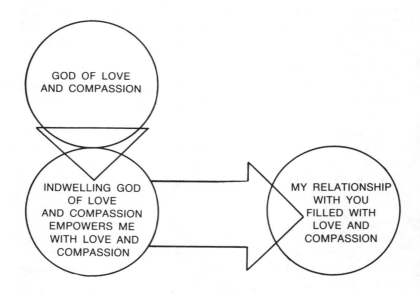

As the child of God learns to respond to the indwelling love of a compassionate Father, his life genuinely takes on the likeness of his Father. He relates to others as he is experientially related to by his Father. This inner transformation is not automatic. It emerges through growth in the reality and appropriation of this love relationship. We not only "love Him because He first loved us,"[6] but we also express our love to others "because He first loved us."

We might ask, "How does God's love change us?"—an important question for us to consider. First, God's personal, intimate love "fills our tanks." Each of us has an inner need to know that we are a person of worth, someone of significance. Warm, caring relationships with parents and significant others are of great help in ministering to this need. We have already seen, however, that vast numbers of individuals never have this need met. They journey through life seeking individuals who will affirm their worth, tell them they are significant, fill their tanks. For some, the tank always seems empty; for others, the tank is only full enough to provide affirmation to cope, but not to live full, productive, joyful lives.

Only one person in all the universe can fill this inner void within us in the absolute sense. That person is the Lord God. When He comes to dwell within us in the intimate sense I have described throughout this chapter, that personal sense of fullness is realized. We know absolutely that we are special, significant, of worth because the Lord of the universe has told us in the center of our being. An emotional warmth fills us that is not only fulfilling, but also liberating.

Thus, the first consequence of God's love is realized internally, personally. A second result follows. Now that the "tank is filled" by God's loving presence, we are freed from the destructive selfishness that causes us to exploit others. With an empty tank, we constantly try to get something from others; with a full tank that God has filled, we quit coercing, manipulating, hounding others to satisfy us. When our own lives overflow with God's presence, joy, and fulness, we have much to give to others and we enjoy giving generously.

I see another consequence of God's love filling our lives. We now have greater capacity to endure others' negative behavior. When someone is harsh, demanding, and manipulative, we don't have to react from our own emptiness. Although we will all experience times of physical, emotional, mental, and spiritual weariness, we are less reactionary to others in need and more able to give lovingly to them when we return to the Lord for renewal.

This truth is seen vividly in the characteristics of love described in 1 Corinthians 13:4–7. I have stated these characteristics in a form that personally highlights the difference in problem and conflict situations when God's love is ministering to us and through us.

God's love gives me *patience* to work for His best solution.

Lack of love makes me face problems impatiently.

God's love gives me *kindness* toward others who see things differently.

Lack of love makes me harsh and unkind to others.

God's love enables me *not to be envious* if solutions benefit you more than me.

Lack of love makes me envy you for getting what I want or need.

God's love enables me *not to brag* about the keen mind, great strength, or better ideas that I have.

Lack of love makes me feel the need to build myself up, to be arrogant.

God's love allows me to be *courteous* and gracious in speech.

Lack of love causes me to be rude, insensitive, sarcastic, or "pushy."

God's love makes me want solutions that will *benefit others*.

Lack of love forces me to be self-seeking, self-centered.

God's love allows me to be *calm*, gentle, not hostile.

Lack of love causes me to anger quickly if weaknesses in my ideas are pointed out, or if "my" solution is not chosen.

God's love helps me *trust* others in problem situations.

Lack of love makes me suspicious of others' motives, actions, statements.

God's love empowers me to be *truthful*, to seek truth above personal advantage.

Lack of love entices me to twist facts, exaggerate, deceive others to win the argument.

God's love helps me *protect* the interests of all.

Lack of love forces me to protect my own interests.

God's love fills me with *hope* for what is good and noble.

Lack of love sees despair when I lose.

God's love enables me to *persevere* in difficult problem situations.

Lack of love has no final hope and so it gives up.

LOVE AND PROBLEM SOLVING

Throughout this chapter, we have explored the dynamic relationship between love and problem solving. Now it would be valuable to consider specific applications of love to problem solving. What difference will the outflowing of God's love make as we encounter daily problems?

It seems to me that only love will build the powerful

context whereby two or more individuals can blend their energies creatively and productively. Only where love exists will individuals feel totally free to let down psychological barriers and defense mechanisms, which stifle maximum productivity. Only where love exists will suspicion and selfishness disappear and the door be opened for a conflict-free environment. Only where love exists will the best solution emerge naturally, spontaneously because the Spirit of God has freedom to guide the participants in an unhindered manner. *Love pays the highest dividends.*

I am impressed with a second powerful personal consequence of love's environment. When the love described in this chapter is guiding our relationship—my relationship with you—we are very conscious of each other. We have heightened sensitivity to our dilemma as we share in the mutual problem. We cannot help being concerned with how the problem is affecting each of us or wanting to know how the other feels. How will the solution impact my life? Your life? What will it cost me? You? Will it enrich your life, or my life? Hurt you or me? Love-motivated problem solving causes us to want well-being for both of us.

The third result flows from the first two. The atmosphere of love guides our communication. We speak to each other with courtesy, not sarcasm, ridicule, belittling, ordering, demanding. We express dignity toward each other because we hold each other in high esteem. Social position, educational advantage, and economic brackets cannot create barriers because with the love of Jesus Christ radiating through our lives, we will refuse to see these temporal facts as giving deeper meaning to our relationship.

D. L. Moody and his associate D. B. Towner were traveling by train to one of Moody's evangelistic meetings. A drunk and disorderly young man boarded the train. He recognized Moody and began to ridicule him. Losing patience, Moody motioned to the conductor and asked him to handle this unruly, offensive man. In a gentle, compassionate manner the trainman took the young man, washed his face, and cared for some bruises he had sustained. When Moody heard what had happened, he felt a personal rebuke. He commented to his companion, "Just think. Only last night I was preaching about the Good Samaritan; yet this morning I find my feet in the shoes of both the priest and the Levite. This trainman's action has served as a rebuke to me from the Lord."

The love of God in Jesus Christ gives us a powerful, distinctive basis for relationships and for problem solving which can be found nowhere else. It challenges all of us to consider how the Spirit of God may want to stimulate new expressions of His love in our lives.

Personal Discovery

1. List the people who are important to you. Beside each name jot down a couple of words from the list below to evaluate the strength of the relationship.

open	closed	strained
one-way	two-way	intimate
supportive	warm	cool
distant	personal	business
argumentative	quality	cliché

2. How high a priority do you place on relationships? Do you see any correlation between your answer and how you cope with problems?

3. Which relationships need to improve? Place a check mark in front of them. What practical ideas from this chapter could be used to work on those relationships?

4. Relationships need to be cultivated to keep them healthy. If we do not enrich them when there are no problems, how can we expect them to hold up in times of tension, misunderstanding, or need? Reflect on your approach to building and maintaining relationships.
   A. How often do you compliment or encourage others?
   B. Do you remember special events in others' lives with cards or phone calls?
   C. When was the last time you initiated a special activity with a person to express your love or friendship?
   D. How open are you to share details of your life that help others get to know you and encourage friendship with you?

5. How would you express love to
   A. a co-worker who gossips about you?
   B. your teenager who dresses in clothes that you dislike?
   C. your spouse who is frustrated with your habit of watching sports, or soap operas, on television every week?
   D. your grandparent who disapproves of your career choice?
   E. your employer who doesn't give you the raise that you deserve?
   F. a neighbor who always borrows and seldom returns items?
   G. a brother/sister who enjoys embarrassing you in front of your friends?

Personal Feedback

1. Talk about how you feel about your relationships with others. Let another person give you feedback as to how he sees you functioning in relationships. Be honest in a positive manner.

2. Describe your relationship to the Lord. In what way would you like this relationship to grow? In what way does your relationship to God help or hinder your relationship to others?

3. "God created us in His image, a personal being unlike all other creatures, and like Him in our unique capacity for relationship. As dependent personal beings, we cannot function fully as we are designed without close relationships. I understand the Scriptures to teach that relationship offers two elements which are absolutely essential if we are to live as God intended: (1) The *security* of being truly loved and accepted, and (2) The *significance* of making a substantial, lasting, positive impact on another person."[7]

In light of the above statement by Larry Crabb, discuss the following questions.
   A. To what extent do you feel security and significance from God?
   B. To whom besides God do you look for security and significance?
   C. Do others ever indicate that you expect too much from them?

Chapter Ten

TWO MODELS: CONFLICT AND PROBLEM SOLVING

What does someone mean when he says of his friend, "Lennie needs some help; he flies by the seat of his pants"? This statement implies that he recognizes his friend's tendency to act without carefully thinking through how he should behave or why he acts as he does. Instead, he impulsively responds to any situation, demand, or crisis by following hunches, feelings, or moods. Sometimes the person may get away with this approach; other times such behavior leads to greater frustration and deeper problems.

Let's examine the role of impulsive behavior in relation to problem solving and conflict. What happens when we don't have a clear understanding of how problem solving and conflict differ? What happens when we have no understanding of what the problem-solving process is, or how to follow it in a knowledgeable way? What happens when we "fly by the seat of our pants" in problem solving?

I was well into adulthood before I realized that no one had taught me an effective approach to problem solving. I had somehow picked up a way to cope with the dilemmas that I faced, but it had occurred quite haphazardly. Was it effective? Was it the best approach? Frankly, I didn't have the faintest idea. I had established some way to solve problems, but certainly it had not been learned in a thoughtful, disciplined manner.

In this chapter I would like to describe two models: one, a model of conflict; another, a model of problem solving.

Each should provide a simple conceptual description for you to interact with. If you have no model, these will serve as a starting point. If you do have a model, these will provide you an alternative to compare to. I believe the models I describe are consistent with what the Scriptures teach. I encourage you to analyze them from this perspective.

To keep the models as simple as possible, I have tried to identify only the essential elements. You may want to add other elements. With the goal of establishing the basics, I find five elements essential to a healthy biblical model.

1. PERSONS in some form of communicative relationship.
2. A PROBLEM that touches our lives in some way.
3. The PERCEPTION that we hold of each other and the problem.
4. God's PRESENCE as an active force shaping the problem and the people.
5. The PROCESS through which the problem solving or conflict must proceed.

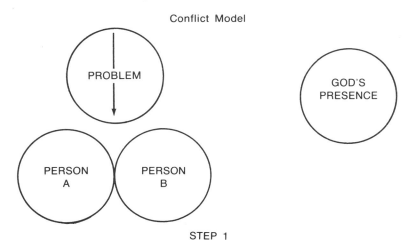

Conflict Model

STEP 1

The conflict model begins with two or more individuals who do not have a *significant relationship* with each other. They may be friends, family members, or work associates and may be friendly with each other, but the friendship is superficial. The fact that their lives do not touch indicates the lack of a significant relationship. The lack of this type of relationship undermines respect, courtesy, and commitment to work through problems mutually and constructively. In addition, because no significant relationship exists, communication is impersonal and superficial. With no setting for meaningful communication, accurate perception is difficult to achieve.

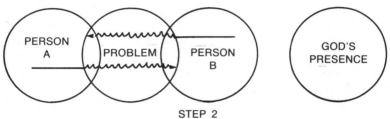

STEP 2

In step two the PROBLEM has entered the relationship. Note that the problem comes *between* the individuals, forcing them apart. PERCEPTION of each other is distorted because each person sees the other *through* the problem. Accurate perception of the problem is hindered because PERSON A cannot clearly see PERSON B's point of view, and vice versa. Since it is difficult to understand the other person's perspective, it is less likely that accurate communication will occur.

Throughout the conflict process God's PRESENCE is experientially left outside the problem situation. The diagram is not suggesting that the individuals do not know God or endeavor to be serious Christians. Yet, ignorantly or unthinkingly they do not invite the Lord's PRESENCE as an essential part of the solution process. Since God is ignored, His resources are not available. Each individual is left to his own skills and knowledge to work toward a solution.

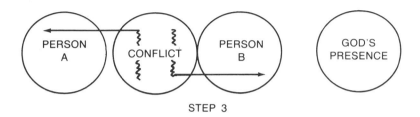

STEP 3

In step three the problem has further separated the individuals. Distortion in perception and communication has led to misunderstanding. The weak relationship has produced less sensitivity to each other, more tendency to attack, belittle, or criticize. The PROCESS, being weak from the beginning, moves in a destructive direction. Individuals are misunderstood and hurt. The problem is left unsolved, or it is solved in a manner benefitting one, penalizing the other.

No model can include every element of the process. I recognize that there are many variations on the model illustrated. For example, some individuals endeavor to have a significant relationship, but through lack of effective problem-solving skills, they ignorantly allow the problem to come between them. In other situations, individuals honestly try to approach the problem in a godly, responsible manner but do not know how to involve God in the process. They end up frustrated, defeated, discouraged.

Problem-Solving Model

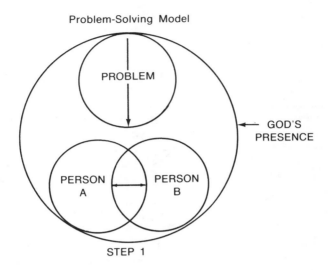

STEP 1

The biblical problem-solving model begins with two or more individuals who place high priority on building a responsible, *significant RELATIONSHIP* with each other. Ideally, the relationship exists before the problem is encountered. Both persons hold their relationship at a higher priority than the problem because they believe the significant relationship gives power for problem solving. Tozer noted, "It is a truism to say that order in nature depends upon right relationships; to achieve harmony each thing must be in its proper position relative to each other thing. In human life it is not otherwise."[1]

Our diagram also shows us that PERCEPTION is more accurate at the outset because the significant relationship gives each person deeper understanding of the other. God's PRESENCE enables each person to practice greater openness and love. His imparted wisdom allows each to perceive the other more accurately. God's PRESENCE is guiding the relationship as a foundation to the upcoming problem.

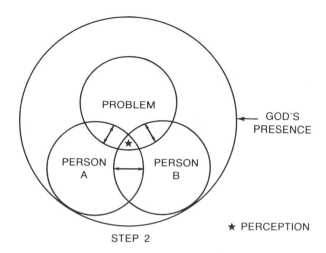

In step 2 the problem confronts each person. *Neither person is willing to allow the problem to come between them and jeopardize the relationship.* Keeping the relationship at higher priority than the problem achieves valuable results. First, the relationship cannot be severed by the problem. Second, communication continues unhindered. Third, PERCEPTION of each other and the problem is more accurate because openness and transparency allows each to see more clearly.

The diagram also indicates that the Lord's guiding PRESENCE has been sought and is permeating the total situation. His wisdom helps each individual see the problem with discernment. His love guards them from suspicion, rudeness, arrogance, or greed. His peace settles each person's spirit and allows clear, accurate thinking. His honor motivates each to manage the problem in a manner giving glory to Him.

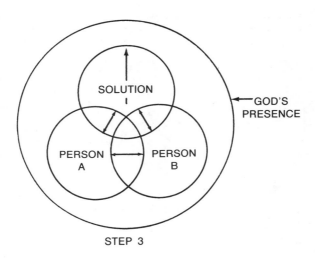

STEP 3

Step 3 leads to an effective solution that strengthens all the individuals involved. In fact, through the problem-solving process each person has profited in some way. The solution is better than any one person could have achieved. And, the relationship has been strengthened because during the process, individuals have affirmed each other as persons of dignity and worth.

The PROCESS, based on biblical principles, moves in a positive, healthy direction and results in a solution that is also positive and healthy. No one feels cheated. Each has contributed his energy to implement the solution because he has been a part of discovering it, and he believes that God is honored in this way.

We do not have to be afraid of problems when we deal with them in a biblical problem-solving way. We know that we will not be ridiculed by our associates, but listened to with respect and dignity. We know that others want to honor God in our mutual effort, and we want that for them.

I believe that the problem-solving process described here is consistent with the nature of God and His interactions with His people and provides a foundation upon which problem-solving skills can be developed. While the actual process will be as creative as the individuals involved, we can observe similar dynamics. The model is appropriate to any situation—in family, church, work, friendships—where His people endeavor to face life creatively, lovingly, and faithfully.

Personal Discovery

1. The following chart will help you identify conflict and problem situations you may be experiencing. Beside each issue put either a "P" to indicate a problem situation, a "C" to indicate a conflict situation, or "N" to indicate that you are not facing a conflict or problem related to that issue. Then write in the name of the person(s) you relate to in the situation: spouse, employer/employee, sibling, church member, roommate, or friend.

Issue	Situation	Person
handling of finances		
noise level		
schedule		
goals		
recreational activities		
choice of friends		
use of other's possessions		

Issue	Situation	Person
amount of time spent together		
care of house/office/ property		
Bible study		
child care and discipline		
authority in decision making		
eating habits		
use of free time		
other (identify)		

2. Choose one situation from the above activity that you marked "P" and one that you marked "C." Diagram them according to the conflict and problem model described in this chapter. Try to see what elements differ in each situation. Then try to identify what changes would be necessary in the conflict situation to make it a problem situation. Be certain to recognize attitudes or actions within yourself that would need to change.

3. Look up the following verses and decide to which of the elements (persons, problem, perception, presence, process) each refers. Some passages may relate to more than one element. Write out specifically what the passage says about the element.

   Romans 12:17–19, 15:1–7
   Philippians 2:1–5

Colossians 3:12–15
James 1:2–5

Personal Feedback

1. I said that I was well into adulthood before I saw that I had not learned an effective problem-solving method (I had learned effective ways to create conflict!). Share what has helped you learn to solve problems effectively.

2. Talk about how we can become more aware of God's presence when a problem or conflict arises.

3. Share an incident from your life in which the problem-solving process described in this chapter was at work.

4. Decide on a current problem or conflict you are facing. Work together to see how each of the five elements from this chapter's models can intersect to create a healthy problem-solving situation. (You may want to share what you have done under exercise 2 of Personal Discovery.)

PART III

PSYCHOLOGICAL DIMENSIONS OF PROBLEM SOLVING

Chapter Eleven

IDENTIFYING YOUR STYLE

What three words would you choose to describe yourself? Every person has his own unique combination of qualities that forms his personality. Just as no two individuals look alike, no two individuals act in the same way. Our personalities are uniquely personal.

When we think of problems and conflicts, we realize that the uniqueness of our personality is an important determinant in how we face them. We know that individuals respond to problems in different ways. While each person's response is personal, it is possible to identify approaches that have similar characteristics.

To help you understand your own style of handling problems and conflicts, I would like you to choose two of the statements below that best describe your approach to problem situations. You may want to choose more than two, but limit yourself to the two that best describe you.

_____ 1. I want to get things accomplished. Achieving goals and meeting needs is important to me. Sometimes it is necessary to force people to accept my solutions. Relationships are not as important to me as getting issues resolved and accomplishing something worthwhile.

_____ 2. I want people to like me. I'd rather not get what I want and keep the peace. I'd rather maintain relationships than get what I want and make someone mad, or hurt his feelings.

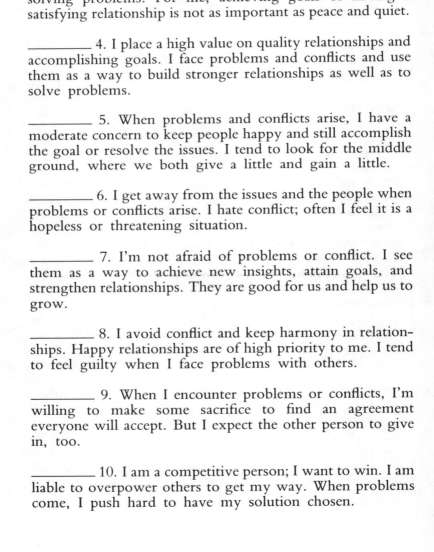

_____ 3. I want to keep peace at any cost. I'd rather avoid conflict, even if it means avoiding people and not solving problems. For me, achieving goals or having a satisfying relationship is not as important as peace and quiet.

_____ 4. I place a high value on quality relationships and accomplishing goals. I face problems and conflicts and use them as a way to build stronger relationships as well as to solve problems.

_____ 5. When problems and conflicts arise, I have a moderate concern to keep people happy and still accomplish the goal or resolve the issues. I tend to look for the middle ground, where we both give a little and gain a little.

_____ 6. I get away from the issues and the people when problems or conflicts arise. I hate conflict; often I feel it is a hopeless or threatening situation.

_____ 7. I'm not afraid of problems or conflict. I see them as a way to achieve new insights, attain goals, and strengthen relationships. They are good for us and help us to grow.

_____ 8. I avoid conflict and keep harmony in relationships. Happy relationships are of high priority to me. I tend to feel guilty when I face problems with others.

_____ 9. When I encounter problems or conflicts, I'm willing to make some sacrifice to find an agreement everyone will accept. But I expect the other person to give in, too.

_____ 10. I am a competitive person; I want to win. I am liable to overpower others to get my way. When problems come, I push hard to have my solution chosen.

Before you read on, look over the ten items again and choose the two that best describe your spouse or another person with whom you face problems or conflicts. Mark down those you chose for yourself and the other person so you will remember them as you read through this chapter.

HOW WE FACE PROBLEMS AND CONFLICTS

In a moment we will look at five styles of relating. Before we begin our investigation, it is important to make some general comments that relate to all five. First, the way we cope with problems and conflicts is a *learned behavior*. As we grew up, we learned to solve, or avoid, problems when we watched others handle problems, especially our parents. Other impressions were gathered by the way others treated us. If we felt overpowered, threatened, or intimidated by others in problem situations, we may have chosen to run away from problems. We also learned to deal with problems by trial and error. Through this "hit and miss" approach, we gained helpful insights related to problem solving, but we also acquired destructive attitudes and skills.

The second point that needs to be underscored is that our personal approach centers around two primary issues: *goals and relationships*. Whatever style we have adopted, we are trying to keep our goals and our relationships with people in balance with our feelings and desires. We have learned through many years of experience how to do this in a way we think is best. We may not always like the way the problem is solved, but it is the way we accept the outcome that maintains our psychological state.

A third issue to keep in mind is that most of us do not use one style in every situation. A number of variables will be identified later that influence which approach we use. Just remember that we probably have one dominant style, which we are most comfortable with. Then we may have one or more back-up styles that we use at other times in different circumstances.

Approach 1—COMPETE: "I'll win no matter who gets hurt."

If you chose statements 1 and 10 in the exercise above, you see yourself as a competitor in problem situations. The competitor needs to *win*. He thinks there are only two acceptable ways to solve the problem: win or lose. And he intends to win if at all possible.

This controlling, aggressive approach is chosen because the individual is extremely goal oriented. In fact, it is so important that the person is willing to sacrifice relationships to gain the solution desired and will employ whatever tactics that achieve desired ends. Though not wanting to admit it, the competitor uses other people to accomplish what he wants, what he deems best. The competitor has a low concern for others' needs, feelings, insights, so he ignores relationships and uses power to gain the goal. Figure 1 illustrates how the competitor resolves the goal-relationship tension.

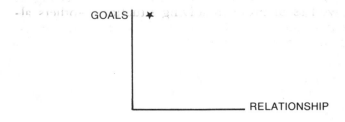

Figure 1

People who use the competitor approach are not necessarily intending to be bad; they can be anyone from the benevolent dictator to the heartless, selfish autocrat. We can expect to see different attitudes and behaviors, but behind all of them, certain issues are the same: The individual controls, manipulates, and overpowers others. The competitor does not believe that others are capable of solving problems. His way is the only way.

Approach 2—WITHDRAW: "I'm leaving; you decide."

If you chose items 3 and 6, you indicated behaviors the withdrawer selects. This person has often been likened to the turtle. When a problem or conflict arises, he retreats to his shell, shutting the world out. Unfortunately, when he escapes, he leaves behind any opportunity to achieve the goal or relate to people.

The withdrawal approach may be chosen for different reasons. Wanting little from life, this person may have adopted a passive lifestyle. The withdrawer may have little desire to achieve and little care for others and may just want to be left alone. Or, a person may select this style because of insecurity, of feeling inferior to others—they are wiser, better, more competent than the withdrawer. When problems arise, this person's sense of incompetence is so strong that he wants to retreat before looking like a fool. Another person may choose this approach because of the feeling of being powerless in problem-solving situations—others always seem to step in and overpower the withdrawer, so retreat is the natural thing to do.

Figure 2

As figure 2 indicates, the withdrawer forsakes both goals and relationships. This individual may physically leave the room saying, "Solve it your own way; just leave me alone!" Or, this person may remain on the scene, become silent, and perhaps stare into space as others undertake a solution.

I do not want to leave the impression that the withdrawer does not like or need people. Such a person may have many friendships, but when problems and conflicts arise, he cannot handle the pressure, so the withdrawer retreats.

Approach 3—SURRENDER: "Protect relationships at all cost."

Items 2 and 8 in the earlier quiz indicate behaviors common to this approach. Approach 3 is used by the person who believes that relationships are of higher importance than needs and goals. Thus, the surrenderer forsakes goals whenever they seem to jeopardize relationships. This person tends to see problems as endangering relationships and so guards from allowing this to happen. The motto: "Avoid conflict at any price; keep the peace."

The person who uses this approach to problem solving and conflict may be revealing underlying insecurity. He may not want to risk offending others or being misunderstood because of fear of rejection. This person's strong need to be liked, to be acceptable, overrides any individual goals. The surrenderer also may be an individual who confuses disagreement with dislike or rejection.

Figure 3

Figure 3 demonstrates how the tension between goal and relationship is resolved by this approach. Protect the relationship at all cost. Surrender goals, needs, wants to keep others happy.

One unfortunate fact about this way of facing issues is that it does not allow the person to be honest with others or self. This individual ignores personal values, insights, and goals, which are lost in the problem-solving process.

Approach 4—COMPROMISE: "Find the middle ground."

When items 5 and 9 are chosen, they suggest that the person uses compromise as the main way of coping with problem situations. The compromiser tries to be a negotiator, a conciliatory person. He believes that everyone has to give a little so all can gain something for the effort. No one wins big, but then no one loses either. Everyone comes out with something.

This approach places priority on realism and flexibility. It endeavors to create an atmosphere of "give and take." The danger behind this strategy is that it may undermine commitment to truth, goals, and relationships. There may be situations in which compromise would be dishonest. Problem situations that involve Christian values or truth cannot be resolved with compromise.

Figure 4

Approach 5—RESOLVE: "I'll build relationships through achieving my goals."

Items 4 and 7 are descriptive of someone who endeavors to help resolve a problem or conflict in a mutually beneficial way. This is the role of the "facilitator," who does not take sides but calls everyone to give his full resources to allow the best solution to emerge. The facilitator works for the good of the total group.

Key ideas underly the "resolve" approach. First is the belief that *both* goals and relationships are important: "Let's build relationships through achieving goals." The "resolve" facilitator attempts to mobilize everyone in solving the problem. He believes that the total group energy will produce more than any one person or segment could achieve. This person believes that everyone can win and refuses to settle for less than the best.

In the field of group dynamics, the term "synergy" has been coined. It describes the combined positive action of each part of an organism, or system, that produces more than that of the individual parts. Interestingly enough, this concept seems to have been on the apostle Paul's mind when he wrote to the Ephesian Christians. He spoke of the church "attaining to the whole measure of the fullness of Christ."

> Then we will no longer be infants, tossed back and forth by the waves, and blown here and there by every wind of teaching and by the cunning and craftiness of men in their deceitful scheming. Instead, speaking the truth in love, we will in all things grow up into him who is the Head, that is, Christ. From him the whole body, joined and held together by every supporting ligament, grows and builds itself up in love, as each part does its work. [1]

Observe that Paul described a process in which every part contributed its full resources to achieve what was best for the whole. It is a principle that underlies the biblical principles of seeking God's glory and the love and well-being of others.

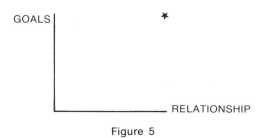

Figure 5

Approach five holds high priority for both achieving goals and building relationships. Differences are welcomed, not feared: "We can express our differences without attacking each other. We can discover answers to our needs that satisfy us all." It requires individuals who are secure within themselves; they hold a high view of others and relate to them with dignity, courtesy, and respect.

VARIABLES INFLUENCING STYLES

I can anticipate a reader thinking that the five styles I have been discussing are rigid personality types, set in concrete. That would be an unfortunate assumption. Some individuals do consistently rely on one style whenever they confront problems and conflicts. Either they feel secure enough with that style to adopt it each time, or they have so thoroughly programmed it into their thought patterns that they automatically rely on it.

As was said earlier, people have a *primary* style with which they are most comfortable. However, a variety of circumstances can motivate them to revert to *back-up* styles that better serve their purposes. To be most effective in coping with problem situations, we should understand some of the variables that influence the choice of style.

This discussion also suggests that no one style is perfect.

Some are better than others, but realistically we all use most of the styles at some time or another when circumstances make it necessary. Most of the time a parent who is already late for work will aggressively solve a problem related to his child rather than take time to involve the child in the total process. After all, the child is already late for school, too!

The setting influences a person's style choice. Many individuals feel more secure in small, intimate groups of friends rather than in large, impersonal groups. In the intimate setting, they feel greater freedom to be open and honest with others and confront them frankly. In the large group, however, these same people retreat into the shell of silence and allow others to suggest solutions.

It would not be uncommon to observe a husband and wife using approach 5 in their interactions at home. Both work together for a mutually satisfying solution. The problem-solving environment they create is warm, positive, open. If we were to observe these same two individuals at church, they might be shy and withdrawn, believing that they are unqualified to interact with others whom they perceive as more educated and "smarter than we are."

The dynamics of the group influence the choice of style. A wife who has an aggressive, competitive husband may surrender to her spouse's demands in solving a problem to keep peace in the relationship. This same woman, however, may find compromise as the most comfortable style in relating to her children. She does not feel overpowered by them and wants to be certain they are treated fairly.

Can you envision a group of people who are typically "turtles" in their approach to problems? They normally withdraw every time. Yet in this setting with other shy, hesitant individuals, some approach problems more boldly, working together to find an answer to their problems.

The strength of the goal being pursued influences style choice. I might ask myself, "How highly motivated am I to achieve the goal? How badly do I want this?" My answer will tell me something about my behavior. If I have set my heart on achieving something, if I want it badly, I will feel more internal pressure to win what I want. It will be hard not to be aggressive, controlling, or even irritated when someone resists my "logic."

A person with a moderately important goal will likely choose a compromising posture to solve a problem or conflict. The person with a minimally important goal will find it easy to withdraw, letting others be responsible for solutions.

I am not suggesting that we choose styles of relating according to the strengths or weaknesses of our desires. I do suggest that people have a limited amount of energy to invest in problem solving. They often do not want to expend intense energy for minimal goals. But it is difficult not to be intense when the goal we are seeking has high personal value.

The strength of relationships influences style choice. Some relationships are so important that a person will not do anything to jeopardize them, especially if the person is not highly motivated toward goals that touch those relationships. The strength of our commitment to the person has much to say about how we choose to relate to him.

My perception of others involved in the problem or conflict influences the choice of style. If we perceive others as being a threat to us, we may retreat out of fear. If we perceive that someone we value is offended by our suggestions, we may be tempted to try and pacify that individual to preserve the friendship. If we perceive that the problem is at an impasse, we may want to seek a compromise to achieve the easiest resolution.

As I have described the variables impacting our styles of relating to other people, I have not tried to describe what *should be.* Rather I am simply stating what *does* happen to people. Few individuals know or take time to stop and ask themselves, "What is happening here? What style of relating should I choose in this situation? Is this style the most effective? Is it what is best for everyone?"

THE "SO WHAT?" QUESTION

So what does all this mean to us? What are we to learn from the discussion of this chapter? What are the implications?

First, I think it is obvious that each of us should attempt to understand these five basic ways people act toward problems and conflict. We should also understand our own basic style and how it is impacting other people and the problems we encounter. Quite frankly, many of us consistently employ problem-solving strategies that are destructive to positive, effective solutions.

Second, approach 5 holds a high view of others and therefore has high value when compared with the rest of the approaches to problems and conflicts. It also calls us to act responsibly toward the problems we face. We need to learn not to be controlled by fear, aggression, or other destructive emotions. The biblical challenge is to allow the Spirit of God to knit us together to find godly answers to our problems. As we relate to one another in love, we honestly desire to share our strengths and receive wisdom and discernment from each other. We are admonished to "speak the truth in love" rather than withdraw from each other, or surrender.

I believe the Scriptures teach this synergistic concept: We unite our energy under the leadership of the Spirit of God and are led to find better solutions than any one of us has. Even our goals and motivations are submitted to God's greater wisdom and purposes. In this way, the spirit of competition or winning gives way to a genuine concern so that others may be built up and God's name may be glorified.

Personal Discovery

1. Look at the two descriptions you chose at the beginning of the chapter. Work through the following questions to help you better understand the implications of your style.
   A. What style do they indicate is most typical of you?
   B. How satisfied are you with this style?
   C. What problems has this style caused you?
   D. What specific steps can you take to improve your way of relating to others?

2. Identify the basic style of relating that your family members, close friends, and work associates use. How does your style impact them? How do they respond to your style? What specific problems have arisen from a conflict of styles?

3. I suggested there are variables that influence the style we rely on most frequently and those we use as a "backup." Review what I have written about the variables. Then jot down ways you use variations on your basic style.

Personal Feedback

1. Ask others to describe the style they observe in you. Share with them your own discoveries and discuss the implications.

2. Discuss how the five styles of relating influence each other. How is each style likely to impact problems?

3. Discuss how you see others when you adopt each style. What does each style communicate to others?

4. Talk about whether you are more goal-oriented or relationship-oriented. Are you satisfied with where you see yourself? How has it impacted your problem solving?

Chapter Twelve

AVOIDING TRAPS TO PROBLEM SOLVING

It's your birthday. A close friend arrives with a beautifully wrapped gift. You immediately sense the excitement in her voice.

"I've got the greatest gift for you! You're going to love it! I can't wait to see the expression on your face when you open the package!"

With trembling fingers you fumble at the ribbon. What is this amazing gift? You are aware of the excitement building within you.

Finally the wrapping is off. You pry the lid off the box and peer inside. Your heart sinks as you gaze upon a gaudy, ugly ceramic vase. You instantly hate it!

What do you say to your thoughtful, excited friend who's certain she's purchased something you will treasure? How can you muster up the false enthusiasm to cover your disappointment? You feel trapped!

Life has many traps. Many cannot be avoided; some catch us so quickly we're snared before we can react; others give ample warning, yet we blunder into them and then curse our stupidity at being caught.

An effective problem solver is perceptive to subtle traps that lead to defeat. In some situations, the trap is within us; in other situations, in the other person. Recognizing and defusing traps is an essential skill the problem solver will want to master.

The traps are called "psychological" traps because they are

rooted in our subconscious. Formed and reinforced over a period of years, they now guide our actions and responses like the rudder of a ship. They are hidden beneath the surface, yet they exert a powerful force that causes us to move this way and that. It is not uncommon to overhear a person say, "I don't know why I set myself up the way I do. I always end up paying for it." Or, "He always manipulates me to get his way. Why do I fall for his schemes every time? I feel like a dummy."

No one is cursed to be an eternal victim of these underground controllers. When we become aware of their existence, we need to realize that the Spirit of God has resources for our liberation. Our responsibility is to (1) discover the truth of God, (2) challenge the enslaving subconscious thought pattern, and (3) seek God's liberating power to free us from destructive habits. Little by little, we will see our outward patterns change as our inner thought processes are renewed.

An effective problem solver is perceptive to these subtle traps that lead to defeat. Recognizing and defusing them is an essential step toward growth in problem solving. Thus, it is important for us to identify the most common traps and discover effective ways to cope with them.

THE POWER TRAP

Superior problem solving demands the total resources of all individuals involved. Unfortunately, many individuals do not believe this. They think that the power to decide what is best resides in them alone. They are to choose; others are to comply.

All of us possess some form of power. In fact, power to effect change is not bad. What is destructive is misused power, power that is exercised *over* others. Usually the power holder controls individuals by forcing them to bow to his demands. Such power may be wielded openly, or subtly, yet the long-term results are destructive.

Power over others may be expressed in a variety of forms, sometimes verbally. A loud, insistent tone effectively intimidates many people. The shy, hesitant person withdraws, giving way to the dominant person. He relinquishes his opportunity to share in decision making though he may feel strongly about the issue at hand.

Power may also be exercised through control of resources. The husband who earns the family's finances may believe that he is entitled to decide how it is to be spent. In his mind, his wife and children hold little or no decision-making power in money use. A Christian who gives large sums of money to his church may feel that he is entitled to more say in how it is spent than less affluent givers.

Power to control is often seen in someone who has perceived or assigned authority. Though the concept of "servant leadership" is commonly talked about in Christian circles, in reality many Christian leaders (parents, husbands, pastors, board members) function as "master leaders." They decide, control, rule over others. Rather than seeing themselves as leaders to help others decide, they manipulate others to make the decisions the leaders want.

Reward and punishment serve as effective means to control others. Though they may be administered openly, many times they are disguised. Either way, the power holder says, "If you do it my way, you'll get these benefits. If you don't do it my way, it will cost you."

Individuals who relate to others by power operate by certain conscious or subconscious assumptions. First, some assume that they deserve preferential treatment. In essence they say, "I'm better, more intelligent, more deserving. Therefore, you should let me 'call the shots.'" Others make the assumption that they are always right; their lives are an ongoing expression of arrogance. The constant message is "I'm right; you're wrong." This assumption causes the individual to look down on others, to brush aside their opinions, needs, or insights.

The third assumption underlying the power seeker's actions is his belief that he has the right to control others. At its worst, this causes him to use other people for his own pleasure or gain. At its best (if there is such a thing), this person wants to be a benevolent dictator, ruling over others as a kindly, but controlling father figure who yet violates human dignity and respect for individuals. Personal growth is stifled, and often a smoldering resentment toward the power holder develops.

Far too many people fall into the power trap when facing problems. Subtle control or manipulation of others is their basic style. Unfortunately, they do not seem to realize that the approach has built-in weaknesses that make it inferior. Consider these weaknesses to the power approach.

One: The power approach cultivates unhealthy relationships. The power holder cannot treat others with genuine dignity and respect. His nonverbal message is "I'm better than you so I must determine the solution to this problem. You are unreliable, undependable, or incompetent." Power holders treat others like children. The adult who is being treated as a child cannot have a healthy view of self because he feels inferior, even incompetent.

Two: The power approach breeds resentment in those being controlled. Individuals created in the image of God intuitively know they were never intended to be manipulated, degraded, or belittled. I am convinced that the discomfort we feel when others do not treat us with respect is a quiet witness that such behavior is wrong. It is a sign of psychological health to be troubled when someone is trying to manipulate us for power-hungry gain.

Three: The power approach destroys the opportunity for teamwork in its most productive form. I stated earlier that all of us possess power in some form. One example is our power to think creatively. When two or more individuals unite to discover the best solution to a problem, the potential to find it is greater than when one is solving it alone. I call this *Power With* in distinction to *Power Over.* As I have used the term, Power Over is a selfish, manipulative, controlling approach to problem solving. Power With is an approach that recognizes power in each individual—power is brought together as a united force to solve the problem in the most productive manner. Power With leaves each individual free to share his resources; each individual comes away inspired and fulfilled because his insights were encouraged, his contributions valued, his worth affirmed.

THE CURSE/CURSE TRAP

Recently I saw a presidential debate between the Republican and Democratic candidates on television. After the debate, a newscaster interviewed the Republican and Democratic campaign chairmen. He asked each what he believed were *his candidate's* strong and weak points in the debate.

The first man mentioned two or three strong points and one area of weakness in his candidate. Then the second man outlined several of the strong points he felt his candidate had made. Then, rather than talking about his candidate's weaknesses, as he had been asked, he began to criticize the opponent in harsh, critical words. I was struck by the fact that he could not resist "cursing" his opponent, even when the newscaster had requested no evaluation.

By contrast, General Robert E. Lee is said to have spoken of a fellow officer in very complimentary words. Another soldier overheard Lee's words and commented that the other officer used every occasion to slander Lee. He expressed amazement that Lee would still speak well of the other man. General Lee replied, "I was asked my opinion of him, not his of me." Though he knew the officer's habit of slandering him, he sought no occasion for revenge.

Most of us fall head over heels into the curse/curse trap. If someone speaks to us in a rude, thoughtless, or unkind tone, we impulsively respond in a similar manner. Inwardly we are saying, "If you think you can do that to me and get away with it you've got another 'think' coming!" The vicious curse/curse cycle has then begun and will foster conflict.

Jesus knew the danger of the curse/curse trap. He spoke about the problem in Matthew 5:43–44. "You have heard that it was said, 'Love your neighbor and hate your enemy.' But I tell you: Love your enemies and pray for those who persecute you, that you may be sons of your Father in heaven." He calls the child of God to a radically different response than He calls the unbeliever. He indicates that we are not to respond to rudeness or hostility with the same response.

Paul expanded this principle in his letter to the Romans. He counseled them to respond to hostility with affirmation. To "bless" someone is to speak well to, or about, them. Paul drew upon Deuteronomy 32:35 to suggest positive actions beyond words. Feed the hungry person; give the thirsty something to drink. [1]

Lest you think this principle is irrelevant to problem solving and conflict resolution, I assure you it has practical significance. The following observations make it clear.

First, individuals encountering problems are often tired, upset, or irritable. Consequently, their speech and behavior are negative. Responding to these persons in a similar way will aggravate the problem. "A harsh word stirs up anger" (Prov. 15:1). If we respond to an irritated person with harshness, we are compounding the problem. God says "Don't respond to harshness with harshness; respond with kindness."

Second, the appropriate response to a "curse" (persecution) is a positive, helpful, constructive action, a "blessing." The response to a proud person is humility; to an evil person, goodness; to a tired, hungry, crabby person, it is a warm, tasty meal served in love.

Third, a positive response to a negative person is the response most likely to defuse his negative emotions, attitude, or behavior. Think about this a moment. When you are "cursing" someone (you are irritable, crabby, angry, unreasonable), what actions from others most likely will ease the tension and solve the difficulty? I know I respond best when someone has the graciousness to be kind, understanding, or compassionate.

Realistically, none of us are always bright, cheerful, and cooperative. When problems occur, we may be in a negative frame of mind. If someone can respond to our "curse" with the gracious love of Jesus Christ, it will more likely

    remind us of the sin we need to confess.

    bathe our tiredness with the spirit of peace.

    defuse our anger with the spirit of gentleness.

    heal a wounded spirit that causes us pain.

THE CLOSED-MIND TRAP

"That will never work."

"We've never done it that way."

"Women are illogical."

"My way is best."

Responses such as those above are characteristic of the closed-mind trap. They describe individuals who face problem situations with their mind in a box. These people are described by this statement: "I've made up my mind; don't confuse me with the facts."

A closed mind is a serious hindrance to effective problem solving. Why, then, would someone act this way?

For some, it is an expression of a stubborn, selfish attitude. Others are threatened by new ideas and fear change, perceiving it as a threat to their security. Some are closed-minded because no one helped them discover the joy of creative exploration.

Whatever the reason, we should all want to avoid the pitfalls of the trap.

What are the marks of a closed-minded person? What

clues do we look for in ourselves, or others, that indicate we are snared by this frame of mind? The list below outlines the dominant characteristics of the closed-minded thinker.

1. Unquestioning attitude, resentment of others who question.

2. Tendency to criticize, attack, reject, or rationalize opposing facts, opinions, or insights.

3. Fear of new or unfamiliar information.

4. Defensiveness when ideas are challenged or opposing facts are mentioned.

5. Spirit of inflexibility, not willing to consider other options.

6. Belief that there is no perspective other than his own.

7. Tendency to magnify the negative and overlook the positive benefits of another's input.

The list makes it apparent that a closed-minded person jeopardizes problem solving. He frequently insists on his solution or opens the door for conflict. Superior solutions are seldom discovered or implemented when the closed-minded person is allowed to dominate.

To suggest an open-minded attitude doesn't mean that we do not subject new or novel solutions to careful evaluation. The open-minded person is committed to find the best solution no matter where it comes from. He is unthreatened by the new, the different, the unusual. He listens with respect to others' ideas. He raises thoughtful questions and welcomes them from others. He expresses a spirit of flexibility and knows that the best solutions usually come as a product of everyone's insights. The open-minded problem solver experiences an anticipation of something better; he welcomes discovery.

I have noticed that upon closer examination the ideas that originally appeared novel, or "far out," have elements that push us to see new aspects of problems, or fresh solutions. Although the unusual idea may need modifying, it opens new horizons for growth and enrichment.

A wise adult determines not to fall into the closed-mind trap or condemn his children to that curse. All of us can listen to ourselves to discover if we are saying

"I want things to stay the same."

"My way is the best way."

"That's impractical."

"What's wrong with what we've got."

"We've never done it that way."

"What will people think?"

THE "I'M NO GOOD" TRAP

Problem solvers not only affirm the potential in others; they also believe in themselves. They have not succumbed to the inferiority trap.

What a tragedy that so much potential is never tapped in individuals. How sad to see intelligent men and women who deceive themselves into believing that they are dumb. One of the most damning characteristics of my childhood and early teen years was the sense of inferiority that persistently hounded me. I am grateful for the day when something within me challenged my fear to explore, and I discovered a power to try new ideas, to encounter the fear of the unknown.

The "I'm no good" trap is not the result of humility or modesty. It is the lie that when God made me He made junk—an inferior product. It is the delusion that says, "I'm dumb; the other person has all the good ideas." When an individual is trapped by this style of thinking, he will not cultivate creative thinking processes, but falls victim to the law of self-fulfilling prophecy.

While teaching in graduate school, I had a student who was highly creative. He said that he began to tap this potential after being in college for some time.

"During my grade-school and high-school years, I was a mediocre student," he said. "Then in college I had an unusual teacher who recognized creative potential in me that I never knew existed. She affirmed what she saw and coaxed me to express it. Slowly it began to emerge."

By the time he had entered graduate studies, the flame was burning brightly. In the years that followed, many people have been enriched by this man's life. Thankfully, he has been redeemed from the "I'm no good" trap.

THE WIN/LOSE TRAP

The single, most destructive snare to mobilizing everyone to achieve the best solution is the win/lose mentality. Unfortunately, it is encouraged by the intensely competitive spirit of our culture. Almost every form of athletic sport is competition-oriented. Winners are rewarded with high bonuses; they receive praise and applause from fans and media. Who wouldn't want to be a winner?

Public education rewards the winner. Individuals endowed with intellectual gifts receive the higher grade, despite the fact that the "C" student may have been more diligent and exerted more effort. My past experience as a seminary professor taught me that the most deserving students do not "win;" often the winners are those who can cram, or stuff, volumes of data into especially absorbent minds the night before the exam. It is a rare teacher who knows how to motivate students to approach learning as a team effort.

When we focus on problem solving, we see again a win/lose approach used in most situations. The common form of decision making in church business meetings is voting, which divides people into opposition forces that attempt to outmaneuver the other to achieve a "win." Psychologically, it creates an opponent situation with each side working against the other, instead of pooling ideas and resources to work together for the best decision.

Since we have been trained to compete in all major events

of society, who should be puzzled that we compete in marriage, family, or other interpersonal situations. Unfortunately, we fail to realize that in the win/lose approach usually *both* parties lose.

— We lose something of our partnership in the mission.
— You lose my energy toward the task because losing makes it harder for me to be motivated to support you.
— We lose the opportunity to pursue together the route to the *best* solution—which is better than mine or yours.

The win/lose trap pits us *against* each other rather than yoking us *with* each other. It's not a matter of semantics. The advantages of combining our resources to discover the best solution are significant. We do not waste valuable energy striving to oppose each other. When we have found the best solution, our motivation is noticeably higher to work together to implement it. Usually, implementing the solution requires less time and less energy since motivation is greater, and the combined forces are available.

The problems that we are challenged to tackle throughout life will demand much energy, which we cannot afford to waste. The psychological traps that have been discussed in this chapter will absorb high levels of energy if we succumb to them. In the process, we will be left worn out, bruised, defeated, and more fearful of facing future challenges. One reason these traps are difficult to cope with is that we are not always able to control the circumstances surrounding the problems we face. For example, the church you attend may practice voting as its basic decision-making process. Whether you like it or not you will find yourself forced to endure situations where you will be pitted against the person sitting next to you in the pew. Thus, we are foolish not to heed the warning signs.

Personal Discovery

1. I have described five traps that hinder effective problem solving. Review each one and decide whether you (a) frequently, (b) sometimes, or (c) rarely are entrapped.
   What does your evaluation tell you about yourself? What steps could you take to avoid the trap(s) to which you're susceptible?

2. Circle the words in the list below that most accurately describe you.

competitive	dominant	fearful	vengeful
resistant	shy	controlling	gracious
winner	team-player	open-minded	independent
listener	manipulator	creative	retaliative
insistant	gentle	traditionalist	tolerant

   What do the words suggest about you and how you face problems? Which words would you like to omit? Which would you like to add? What specific steps would you implement to release yourself from the traps you tend to fall into?

3. Look up the following verses and write down what they suggest about the curse/curse trap. What do you learn about helpful and harmful responses? Proverbs 15:4, 13, 23, 28; 16:24; 18:13; 20:5, 22; 22:11.

4. What factors cause an individual to adopt a closed-mind attitude? How does this reduce the effectiveness of problem solving? What advice would you give a person who wanted guidance in becoming more open-minded?

5. What relationships are you involved in where you or someone else tries to overpower others? Which relationships are basically win/lose-oriented? What could you do to change these dynamics?

Personal Feedback

1. Discuss how our society promotes power as an approach to problem solving. Consider educational status, age, finances, physical strength, gender. Think of how these are at work in your life.

2. Discuss: I am liable to be closed-minded when . . .
   I feel "I'm no good" when . . .
   I want to retaliate and "curse" others when . . .
   I try to win when I'm around . . . and usually when I'm around . . .
   I use power to control others when . . .

3. Try to identify people and events from your past that have taught you unhealthy approaches to problem solving. Share them and discuss what their impact is on you now.

Chapter Thirteen

EMOTIONAL DIMENSIONS OF PROBLEM SOLVING

The phone rings. It's your friend Sue. Her voice trembles with emotion. "Roberta, Todd is at it again and I can't handle it. He won't obey me; in fact, he laughs at me when I tell him I'm going to punish him. What am I going to do? Sometimes I think I'm going to lose my mind!"

After ten minutes of conversation, you hang up the phone. As you think back on what Sue said, you realize how emotional she was. You sensed her feelings of frustration and despair, and once you heard her sob. Then something happened inside you; you wished you could reach out and hold her to express your compassion and support. Now you realize that you, too, have been touched emotionally by the conversation and Sue's plight.

The imaginary scene I've painted is not unrealistic. In fact, just before writing this chapter, I was in a phone conversation with a person who was describing her relationship with a friend. She was describing her feelings for this person who was going through a very stressful time. Then she said something like this: "I don't know how many people I've talked with in the past few days who were crying out for help in some kind of difficulty they are experiencing."

Few of us encounter problems and conflicts in an unemotional manner. Rather, we experience the range of positive and negative emotions that are associated with success and failure, growth and defeat.

MAN AND HIS EMOTIONS

Man is an emotional being. Emotions permeate our total life experience. God has enriched our lives with the capacity to feel, to flavor, to sense every dimension of life. Emotions bring excitement, delight, and awe to many daily events, as well as introduce us to sadness, loneliness, despair, and grief.

Recently, a couple told me that they wanted to do something special for our family. I shared this exciting news with my family; however, I did not tell what the special event would be so it would be a surprise. At least once a day now someone asks me something about the "surprise." I sense in each family member the anticipation, the eager expectation of this unknown blessing. Simply saying "Something special is going to happen to the Wakefield family" has stimulated emotions in all of us.

The Lord intended for the emotional dimension of our lives to enrich us. His purpose was to give depth and flavor to our experiences. Unfortunately, sin established a foothold in our lives and created confusion, distortion, and imbalance in our emotions. Many individuals are either too out of touch with important emotions that could enrich their lives, or have emotions that harass them unmercifully.

Our emotions are an integral part of us, a significant dimension of our maturity or immaturity. To be a fully functioning adult, we need to have the capacity to respond emotionally with normal, wholesome responses. Some adults never achieve a healthy level of emotional maturity.

What does it mean to have emotional health? What are some indications that we are emotionally mature?

The emotionally healthy individual has the capacity to establish warm, positive relationships with others. This person is comfortable when he gives more than receives. The healthy individual expresses love as compassionate concern for others and consistently relates to others in a manner that is satisfying to self and others, not destructive to relationships.

The emotionally healthy individual is able to cope with negative or destructive emotions in a constructive manner. He does not deny anger, but discharges it in an appropriate, nondamaging way. Harmful emotions do not spill out randomly and pollute relationships.

The emotionally healthy individual is not ruled by tension, anxiety, or fear. This person knows how to face changes without undue threat or resistance. He can cope with differences in others without becoming hostile, demanding, or frightened. When unforeseen circumstances occur, the emotionally healthy person is not immobilized with fear or anxiety.

The emotionally healthy individual is realistic. He does not need to escape into a dream world or use defense mechanisms that hinder relationships and cause a person to put off facing the truth. Even when the truth is not pleasant to face, the emotionally mature individual will face it responsibly.

FACTS ABOUT EMOTIONS

All of us are born with the capacity to feel. While all emotional responses are not seen in the newborn child, he has all the resources to allow each emotion to emerge at the appropriate time in the developmental sequence. If the environment is basically healthy, the child's emotions will be affirmed when they begin to emerge, and the child will feel comfortable expressing them.

The first fact we note is that most of our emotional responses are learned through experience and the culture in which we are reared. Each family creates its own environment for the child to come to maturity. Beyond the walls of the family, the child encounters a larger community, which enriches or undermines the family teaching and encourages other emotional responses. Significant relationships with strategic individuals can have incredible impact on the growing person's emotional development.

Not all children grow in a healthy environment. Some children are taught early in life that emotional responses are unacceptable. Most boys are taught that "boys don't cry," so they repress the yearning to cry and grow into adulthood unable to weep, even when it is in their best interests. Other children are taught that any expression of anger is sinful. Since they have no valid means to express anger, they turn it inward, causing them much harm in the years to come.

Some children grow in an environment that stimulates emotions excessively. They do not learn to control emotions appropriately or to use appropriate ways to direct their emotions. They may even be encouraged to overreact with emotions either by outright teaching ("If he does that to you again, punch him in the nose!") or by the parent's own example of uncontrolled emotions.

A second important fact about emotions is that they are complicated. As many as four hundred different emotional responses have been identified. With such a high number of possibilities, the chance of mislabeling emotions is great. When an individual mislabels the emotion he perceives in another, this mislabeling can lead to an inappropriate response on the labeler's part or a negative judgment when it is not valid. One of the basic problems in relationships is the failure to perceive important emotional clues in the other person and so miss using these to enrich the relationship through showing compassion, empathy, or concern.

The third fact relates to the power of emotions. Probably the greatest value of emotions is the motivation for life they give us. Emotions are the underlying power source that energizes our actions. The words we use illustrate this. Can you recall someone saying something like this?

"I'm so excited I can hardly sit still!"

"I'm so angry I could spit nails!"

"I'll make the team if it kills me!"

The person's emotional state is expressed in a desire to be active, to release energy. Not all emotional responses are spoken of so openly or vividly. Some hide like underground streams, powering outward actions to fulfill some inner goal, dream, or desire. These can be positive or negative emotions. A parent's love for a child may be the energizing force needed to work diligently and provide security for the coming years. On the other hand, resentment that the child had been born could generate a constant barrage of criticism against the child.

Although I have emphasized the power of emotions, some emotions have the opposite effect and actually drain the individual of energy. Here are a few illustrations.

"I'm so discouraged I'd like to quit."

"My depression has left me with no energy."

"He has so much grief he doesn't even want to go to work."

Since emotions are a primary motivator, we need to realize that we may not know why people are acting as they are. Many of the reasons people do things are based on their emotions, and those emotions may not be outwardly evident. I recall being part of a decision–making group. A decision was called for that appeared uncomplicated; however, a friend was incredibly resistant to a proposed solution. Frankly, I was puzzled and irritated at his odd behavior. We left the meeting with a high level of stress. Later that evening my friend phoned me and shared facts unknown to me. He had had a negative experience with an individual in a similar situation (though that individual had nothing to do with our problem). His fear of what might occur in this situation was based on his past experience, of which I had no knowledge. I would have remained puzzled if he had not been thoughtful enough to tell me the details.

HOW EMOTIONS IMPACT PROBLEM SOLVING

You may already sense that our emotions are a strategic element in how we face problem situations. They can be an asset or a liability, generate energy to motivate us or become painful stumbling blocks to progress. We cannot ignore the impact of our emotions on problem solving. To do so leaves us ignorant of a crucial element in the process.

Emotions impact problem solving because *we communicate by emotions,* as well as by thoughts (cognitively). Most of us overlook this basic principle and get into trouble. In the previous illustration, I failed to consider underlying emotions that could be coloring what my friend was saying and came away confused. But when a person is responding from his emotions, it will often defy logic or reason. Therefore, in many situations we are confused, irritated, or angry about what others are saying or doing because it seems so illogical. *When people communicate from their emotions, it is frequently not based on reason.*

Our second observation is closely related to the first. Since our emotions cannot think, we cannot expect them to act rationally. Emotions must be under the control of our cognitive (thought) processes to achieve healthy results. A person "feels" the decision he wants and responds toward others with that feeling, which creates difficult situations for problem solving. While the emotion is sending input to the mind subconsciously, the person is not consciously aware of this hidden motivation.

An alert, observant person can pick up valuable clues that indicate the presence of hidden emotional motivation. It may be revealed through body language (posture, facial expression, movement), speech patterns, or vocal intensity; however, the skilled communicator will avoid making quick decisions. Rather, he will feed back his observation to the other person and seek a confirmation of it.

Even though emotions cannot think, they can influence problem solving. Emotions have power—power to impact decisions, whether good or bad. Since emotions are usually thoughtless energizers, they must be under the leadership of our cognitive processes to assure healthy, effective decisions.

Observe a note of caution here. No reader should interpret what has been said as an indication that our emotions are a nuisance to problem solving. Emotions are valuable *sensors* that cue us in to issues that might escape our cognitive view. These sensors tell us of subconscious data of which we are not consciously aware. In this way emotions play an invaluable role in perceiving data that the conscious process may overlook.

A third observation must be stated: *Undirected emotions can be dangerous to problem solving.* You may have already picked this up from the earlier discussion, but it is too important not to state forcefully. The writer of Proverbs recognized this truth and often spoke of it. Notice these examples of his concern for unbridled emotions.

"A hot-tempered man stirs up dissension."[1]

"A harsh word stirs up anger."[2]

"A perverse man stirs up dissension."[3]

"Drive out the mocker, and out goes strife; quarrels and insults are ended."[4]

In each reference the writer links uncontrolled, negative emotion to dissension and quarreling. The feelings involved need not be intense, or openly hostile; they may be subconscious feelings of insecurity, loneliness, insignificance. Still, they will jeopardize a healthy problem-solving process.

The fourth point has been discussed but needs to be emphasized in its own right. *Repressed emotions influence problem solving.* We can be blinded *by* our emotions, and blinded *to* them. When we ignore repressed emotions, they thwart the smooth, free flow of ideas and hinder the process that leads to productive solutions. One of the common deterrents to effective solutions is hidden emotions, which erect barriers to productive relationships and effective solutions. The term "hidden agenda" is used in group dynamics to describe these culprits that are not openly recognized, but significantly influence what is happening in the group. Repressed emotions are a major form of "hidden agenda."

COPING WITH EMOTIONS

If emotions are the powerful factor in problem solving that I have indicated, how are we to respond to them? How can they benefit us, not harm us? How can they enrich the process, rather than jeopardize it?

Five suggestions can be given to help harness emotions and direct them toward constructive ends. While the suggestions can be stated simply, a person may have to invest considerable time becoming skilled in applying them. Proficiency will require practice.

Monitor your emotions before, during, and after problem solving. Actually, we need to monitor two processes at the same time. We must be in touch with ourselves both cognitively and emotionally. Since problem solving is largely a thinking process, the bulk of the time will be spent on the cognitive track; however, we should frequently switch to the "feeling" track and check in with our emotions. "What am I feeling right now?" By maintaining this ongoing checkup, we will become aware of any subconscious feelings that are pushing their way into our thought process.

Notice that I'm suggesting that the monitoring actually begins *before* we come to the problem–solving stage. We can ask ourselves, "Am I aware of any feelings that I am carrying into this situation?" "What has been bothering me that I am feeling emotionally concerning the issue I'm facing?" By raising these questions in advance, we do not carry them into the process and create obstacles for ourselves and others.

An executive recently told me of an important board meeting he attended. The night before, he slept poorly. He came to the meeting in a "crabby" mood. As we talked about the situation, he realized that during the meeting his irritable attitude infiltrated his communication. He began to see how helpful it would have been to himself and other board members if he could have identified his negative emotions and dealt with them in a positive manner.

The Scriptures indicate that we can conduct a cognitive assessment of our feelings to understand our emotional state. We are instructed to

> Get rid of all bitterness, rage and anger, brawling and slander, along with every form of malice. Be kind and compassionate to one another, forgiving each other, just as in Christ God forgave you.[5]

This assessment can be done prior to meeting with others, or during the time we are together working on a problem. Monitoring our emotional state is an invaluable way to deal responsibly as a team member.

Monitor the emotions of other individuals you are working with. This requires competence in identifying clues that others give us. We will need skill in *listening and watching* for indications of emotional issues in others. We need to be cautious, however, not to predetermine what the emotion is that we sense. The other person is the authority on his emotions. We are responsible to feed back what we observe, allowing the other person to document what he is actually feeling.

> Concentrate especially on reflecting *feelings*. It is not enough to hear the other's emotions; they need to be understood and accepted. Sometimes the diatribes of the other will seem like a deliberate attempt to hurt you, and you will be tempted to strike back in rage. If you choose to resist that impulse and empathically reflect the other's feelings, you will be amazed at how quickly the other's feelings usually subside.[6]

This basic communication skill is often ignored; the problem-solving process is weakened.

Focus first on the emotional aspects of problems or conflicts. Then they will not be dragged through the entire process, creating a needless resistance and jeopardizing the potential for a healthy solution. Whenever you realize the possibility for anger, resentment, fear, insecurity, mistrust, or rejection, help the individuals involved work through these emotions before focusing on the problem to be solved.

After his many years as a consultant, Robert Bolton has made this observation.

> Many approaches to conflict resolution stress the importance of *rationally* examining specific issues at the outset. My experience suggests that this should usually be the second step. *When feelings run high, rational problem solving needs to be preceded by a structured exchange of the emotional aspects of the controversy.*[7]

Recognize that problems have an emotional, as well as cognitive, dimension. Previously I said that we need to identify emotional issues that precede the problem-solving process. Now I am suggesting that during the process, people function not only in the cognitive realm; we are unified persons, involving ourselves both rationally and emotionally. We both think and feel.

When an individual realizes that he comes to problem situations as a unified person, he will respect the impact of emotions on the process. He will be less likely to ignore the emotional input that is occurring within himself and in the process. He will understand that achieving a solution involves both an emotional and rational action.

Recognize that you must talk to a person's emotions as well as his intellect. When we talk to a person's intellect, we stimulate thought, generate ideas, cultivate insight. When we talk to his emotions, we touch the power base of his inner life. Appealing to one's emotions will more quickly achieve action than appealing to his mind, since greater motivation comes through the emotions.

One of the most practical ways to relate to another person's emotions is through empathy, identifying with the other's emotion. It is as though we put ourselves in that person's place, perceiving as that person perceives, feeling as that person feels. Of course, we cannot do this completely, but when we communicate empathy, the person realizes that we have taken the time and have the compassion to understand life from his perspective. The person is much more likely to respond positively to us and become a cooperative team member.

We cannot fully understand problem solving without coming to grips with its emotional dimension. It is tempting to see the process only as a rational process; however, to do so is a fatal error, which will lead ultimately to disappointment since that is only one aspect of the total process. In summary, an individual functions both as an emotional and rational being. Competent problem solvers respect this principle.

Personal Discovery

1. The effective problem solver understands his own emotional make-up. He knows how his emotions influence his view of problems, how his emotions impact others, and how theirs impact him.

   To get a better perspective on your emotions, complete the following chart. Place a check mark in the column that tells how often you express that emotion.

	Often	Occasionally	Never
Affection toward others			
Joy			
Tenderness			
Boredom			
Embarrassment			
Shame			
Anxiety			

	Often	Occasionally	Never
Frustration			
Excitement			
Loneliness			
Sadness			
Anger			
Jealousy			
Fear			
Guilt			
Silliness			
Inferiority			
Peace			
Apathy			
Awe			
Arrogance			
Sexual desire			
Bitterness			
Pride			
Shyness			
Thankfulness			
Neglect			
Enthusiasm			

2. Using the above checklist, think through the following
    questions as a way to understand how your emotions
    relate to the problems and conflicts you encounter.
    A. Which of your emotions help you solve problems?
    B. Which of your emotions hinder problem solving?
    C. Which of your emotions encourage conflict?

D. How do your emotions impact relationships, especially during problem situations?

E. What emotions in others elicit a negative response in you? How does this negative response influence problem solving?

3. Review the key points of the chapter to discover the insights that are especially relevant to you. Write out each one as it applies to your relationships with people and problems you face. Be specific. For example, "When I talk with Emily I become defensive because I'm fearful that she will find fault with me. I can see that I am repeating a pattern that I used in coping with Mom when I lived at home."

Personal Feedback

1. Using the chart under question 1 of Personal Discovery, complete the evaluation of how you see *each other*. Complete the evaluation before you share the results. Describe how you see the other person's emotions affecting problem solving. Try to give feedback that will help each person understand himself better.

2. Talk about emotions that are hindering your relationships with others. Look those emotions up in a concordance to find biblical counsel about coping with them.

3. Decide whether you agree or disagree with the following statements. Discuss them to see if you can come to agreement on the wisest course of action. Be certain to include biblical insights that may apply.

A. One of the best ways to cope with anger is to admit it to the other person.

B. If two individuals cannot settle an argument, it is best to leave it for another day.

C. Most people *learn* to worry and can *learn* not to worry.

D. My emotional health is directly related to my trust in God.

E. I never have to be repeatedly defeated by any emotion; I can learn new ways to respond appropriately.

PART IV:
PRACTICAL SKILLS FOR
PROBLEM SOLVING

Chapter Fourteen

"CREATING THE SETTING"
SKILLS

When I was a child I determined that if I ever married, I would never argue with my wife. Years later, I found myself married and not able to live up to my determination. The reason was not because Winnie, my wife, was so difficult to get along with. Rather, I had never been taught communication or problem-solving skills with which to face problems and resolve differences. When I entered this new phase of my life, I was not equipped with the resources to live up to my convictions.

Problems would pop up suddenly, and before I knew what had happened, we were in a heated argument. We'd exchange sharp words, anger would flare, and we would lose control of the situation. When I finally cooled down, I'd feel guilty and ashamed of my behavior. I would determine not to allow it to happen again, but like it or not, eventually the same scene would recur. I felt powerless to break the vicious cycle. I'd say to myself, "This is maddening! I resolved not to let this foolishness occur, and yet here it is tormenting us again."

Many of you readers identify with what I am "confessing." You have no difficulty visualizing scenes that occur in your house that you never planned. Before you know what has happened, the heated argument has exploded in full force. It finally ends with both parties exhausted, defeated, and ashamed—a bitter experience for everyone.

Is there any hope for breaking this victimizing pattern?

Can we develop skill in heading off these unproductive, frustrating scenes? I'm happy to state a clear yes to these questions. In this chapter, let's attack one of the root problems and study ways to evaluate the setting where our problems arise. In making the evaluation, we are able to suggest several ways to create a positive setting for problem solving.

Problems and conflicts always occur in context; that is, certain circumstances surround the problem. Often by changing those surrounding circumstances, we radically influence the outcome of the problem. We can determine the setting for problem solving, or we can leave it to chance. We are wise to choose the most productive ground upon which to face our problems.

CREATE A POSITIVE ENVIRONMENT

Let's raise several questions that can help us think through the difference between a positive and negative environment. By the word "environment" I mean anything around and within us that will impact the problem-solving process. We want to find out how we can make the environment work for us, not against us.

When you encounter a problem, learn to ask yourself, *"Is this the appropriate time to solve this problem?"* Asking this question is not an effort to avoid dealing with the issue, but an honest appraisal of the *timing* for effective interactions. It is no sin to postpone resolving a problem if a later time is needed.

Examine these problems and decide when is the best time to solve them.

1. You've arrived home from work very weary. Your spouse is in the kitchen preparing supper. Your eighteen-month-old child is crying in the crib. You notice that the living room is a mess and begin to feel irritated at your spouse.

2. Your son is watching his favorite professional football team on television. You want to talk to him about a failing grade on his report card.

3. Your husband tends to be an impulsive buyer. It is Christmas Eve, and you happen to look through the checkbook. You notice that the account is overdrawn.

Each of the situations I've identified may reflect a valid concern; however, attempting to solve the problem at that time is a poor risk. The environment is set up to work against resolving the issue. Either the matter is not that critical an issue (messy living room), or not in need of urgent solution. The issue of the report card can wait for a couple of hours. Your financial dilemma will wait until after Christmas day.

Another question to ask is *"What is our emotional state?"* In the first illustration I gave, the person is physically exhausted. This will create a situation for most individuals in which their emotional threshold is low, making them vulnerable to expressing harmful feelings. As John Powell wisely observes,

> While my emotions are throbbing with these fears, angers, and self-defensive urges, I am in no condition to have an open-minded, honest, and loving discussion with you or with anyone else. I will need . . . emotional clearance and ventilation . . . before I will be ready for this discussion.[1]

We may need to flush out negative emotions before we can enter into a problem-solving situation with someone else; otherwise, we will carry these into the relationship and jeopardize the outcome. These emotions can be released in several ways. We can pray (not to get the other person straightened out, but for help in coping with our emotions). We can write out our feelings as a way to release them and better understand how they are impacting us and the problem. We can exercise. Going for a walk may help us relax and think through our feelings.

I have found it helpful to ask, *"What will distract us?"* Distractions may be external or internal. External distractions include such things as the sound of a radio or the sight and sound of a television set. Even the visual distraction of people moving about can make it difficult to concentrate. The noise of children playing, or crying, will make the task of problem solving more difficult. Internal distractions include anything that keeps coming into our minds, interfering with our concentration.

We may need to physically move to another location or rid the present location of the distractions. Internal distractions may be more difficult to remove, requiring rest, completing what is unfinished mentally, or learning how to set it aside to concentrate on the problem before us.

I find that inviting the other person to go for a walk while we discuss the problem is often helpful. Or, I may suggest that we discuss the problem over a meal at a restaurant if the problem is not too severe. These more informal, relaxed settings are frequently productive for mutual problem solving.

It is important to ask ourselves, *"Is our appearance and manner positive?"* If we have anything that is offensive, anything that will hinder our relationship, we need to remove it. Presenting ourselves in a pleasant, friendly, pleasing manner will encourage the other person to think well of us and to feel more comfortable in our presence.

CREATE A POSITIVE ATTITUDE

When speaking about good and evil men, Jesus said that "out of the overflow of his heart his mouth speaks."[2] I have been impressed with the wisdom of this statement. Often the words we speak are prompted by underlying issues within us that we may not be aware of. For this reason I have found it essential to reflect on my inner state as I prepare to face an issue with someone else.

When you anticipate coping with someone else over a difficult problem, prepare yourself by prayer and reflection. Ask the Lord to give you insight into your motives, your emotions, and your basic attitude toward the individual and the problem. Invite the Lord to bring you to oneness of heart and mind as you work together with this person.

During this time of prayer, allow time for self-examination. Try to discern whether you will come to the situation with a healthy spirit. Do you know of unresolved factors that will hinder your working with others? Are you aware of anything that you are sensitive about? What might another say that would "set you off"? How could you prepare yourself for such possibilities?

Create a positive attitude by thinking through what might be upsetting to the other people with whom you will be relating. What may they fear from you? How could you communicate a spirit of good will and harmony with them? What could you do to help them form a positive mental attitude?

Often simple statements that express trust and support are invaluable in setting the stage for productivity. When others know that we care about their well-being, they become less fearful and more cooperative. When we communicate trust, we build bridges that allow us to move back and forth across the turbulent waters of communication.

DEVELOP CLEAR PROCEDURES

One common error many people make is to enter into problem solving with no clear procedures. Since they have not discussed how they will proceed, the process then unfolds haphazardly and increases the chances for disaster to occur. When procedures are lacking, the parties involved do not know how to work together. Each tends to establish his own plan without communicating it to anyone else.

In a later chapter, I will outline a problem–solving process that you can use. For now it is sufficient to emphasize that all parties involved need to agree on a clear statement of the problem. Then they need to determine how they will proceed to work toward an effective solution.

In preparation for problem solving, we need to determine what information we have to bring to the process. As we reflect, we may realize that we need to do more research to gather more data. Poor preparation will hinder the process.

SEEK COMPETENT ASSISTANCE

At some time we all encounter problems that require others' assistance. We may be able to solve most of them, but few of us are able to handle all of them without help from others. Unfortunately, many people believe that it is a mark of weakness to turn to others, which leads them to stumble and fumble through their problems and see them blossom into serious conflicts. Still, they will not seek outside help but reap a harvest of pain, defeat, and disaster.

A wise person knows when a problem is too difficult to face alone. A person of wisdom *and* humility seeks the counsel and guidance of others. The Bible clearly teaches that God has placed others in His family who have gifts and insights to enrich our lives. We are foolish not to receive God's grace through fellow believers.

We may need help from others in three ways. First, we may need their assistance to strengthen or repair our relationships. We may realize this at the beginning. It is far better to see that we do not have the relational resources to cope with our problems and conflicts than to create unnecessary interpersonal damage that will be costly to repair.

Second, we may need the assistance of others to guide us through the problem–solving process. We may not have developed the skill ourselves. Or, the problem may be so intense that we cannot process the information, sort out our feelings, and maintain the relationships all at the same time.

Thus, we may invite a competent person to undertake this task.

Third, we may seek the help of others if we do not have the necessary information to solve the problem. The problem may require special data not available to us. If we see this need at the beginning, we will avoid frustration and delay by finding the person who can give us the necessary facts; otherwise, we will be functioning on "pooled ignorance," which often leads to confusion.

Competent assistance does not necessarily mean a professional counselor. A competent person is anyone who can fulfill the task we need. We need to ask, "Who do we know that is competent to help us with our need?" We might find help in another family member, a friend, or a work associate.

I recall a time when our family was facing a painful, complex interpersonal problem. Each of us was trying to act responsibly, but we were enmeshed in the situation. We asked three individuals from our church family to guide us through the problem-solving process. None of the individuals were church staff members. They were loving Christian friends whom we respected. We knew they would seek to be impartial and seek the mind of the Lord. They guided us through the process in an effective, loving manner. We will always be grateful for their ministry to us.

By contrast, I have known many husbands who would not seek help from a counselor because they saw it as a threat to their ego. Instead, they adopted a macho "I don't need any help" attitude, which led to further hurt, and too often, to divorce.

CREATE THE SETTING

By now I hope you realize that there is much we can do to prepare ourselves for problem solving. We can become skillful in creating a productive environment. We can become competent in setting the stage for fruitful interpersonal relationships. We can be wise in spotting elements in the environment that will cause us to bog down or go astray. These "setting" skills are available to each of us. We are foolish not to become skilled in using them, because all of us need them in facing life's difficult situations.

Personal Discovery

1. To help you identify patterns that may have developed in your life, work through the following questions to sharpen your skills of creating the setting.

    A. At what time of day do I encounter recurring problems?

    B. What is my usual emotional state at this time of day?

    C. What is my usual emotional state when I face problem-solving situations?

    D. Where am I most likely to solve problems? What specific room or setting?

    E. Where do I most frequently encounter conflict? What specific room or setting?

    F. What rooms in my home, work, or other settings have many distractions, or are ineffective settings for problem solving? How or where could the setting be changed?

    G. What is my common attitude toward problems, and how do I convey this attitude to others that are involved?

    H. Do I consciously try to create a healthy environment for problem solving? If not, what should I begin to do?

2. Review your answers to the above questions. Look for insights that will help you sharpen your "setting" skills. Look for patterns that impact your problem-solving

strategy. Which patterns are negative? Which are positive? Try to decide where changes would be especially profitable. Be specific about changes that will sharpen your "setting" skills.

Personal Feedback

1. Share examples from your own experience in which poor settings hindered problem solving. Think of settings that fostered conflict.

2. Talk about *when* you are most conducive to solving problems. How successful are you at choosing the most appropriate time?

3. Think about the primary people with whom you face problems. Identify them by name. How skilled are you at noting their emotional state? Talk about how a person *accurately* discerns another's readiness to solve problems.

Chapter Fifteen

PERSPECTIVE-TAKING SKILLS

Many of us have the tendency to "romanticize" biblical events. We think that Daniel had a delightful night in the lions' den. We forget that it was a stinking, dirty place with nowhere to sleep comfortably. God protected him, but the Bible doesn't say that he provided a waterbed, air conditioning, and a morning shower!

Or, what about Noah? Do you imagine that he spent day after day in the ark with a sense of peace and tranquility? Actually, he had a major task feeding and watering the creatures and cleaning out the pens. Even the environment wasn't that great. Outside it was raining; inside, probably dark and damp. That's not my idea of a vacation!

Why is it hard for us to have an accurate picture of others' experiences? Why do we overlook their hardships, their trials, their disappointments? Why do we approach misunderstandings with the tendency to assume that the other person is deliberately trying to be mean, hateful, or rebellious?

We are generally weak at seeing another's perspective—life through their eyes. Look at the cartoon in figure 1. Imagine the character as a fourteen-month-old girl. Let's look at life from her perspective. She is trying to open the door. Notice she has to reach *up* to get the doorknob. We would reach *down*. Her muscles are not strong, so it is difficult to grasp the knob securely and twist it with much force. Opening a door is not easy for our fourteen-month-old child.

Figure 1

Let's expand our perception of the child. Pause after each question and think about what it's like to be that age.

What's it like not to be able to see what's on the table because you're too short?

What's it like to have someone get mad at you because you messed in your pants, when you have no control over it?

What's it like to have poor muscle control? You reach for the glass of milk but knock it over because your muscles don't "steer" your hand accurately.

What's it like to be hungry but be so limited in speaking that no one can understand what you want?

I could go on describing situation after situation, but you probably begin to see the picture. We seldom stop to consider what life is like for others. Yet, the ability to enter into another's world, the capacity to empathize with that individual, to demonstrate true understanding of needs, dreams, hurts, is powerful in communicating love. Dr. Elton Mayo is quoted as saying, "One friend, one person who is truly understanding, who takes the trouble to listen to us as we consider our problems, can change our whole outlook on the world."[1]

You can develop the skill of perspective taking—the ability to perceive another person's world more accurately, more completely. No one except God can fully understand how others feel, think, or perceive; however, we can increase our skill in this area and reap sizeable benefits for ourselves and others. Although I am exploring this subject with you as an essential aspect of problem solving, it is important for you to see this skill in a larger context. You can practice perspective taking in any relationship as a ministry of love. Few people take time to understand others; nevertheless, when we find an individual who does, we feel loved.

Here a word of caution is needed. Skills are most effective when they flow from healthy attitudes; otherwise, the skill can be a manipulative tool to get our own way. The perspective-taking skill rests on the conviction that all people have worth and deserve to be treated with dignity and compassion. Our little fourteen-month-old child rates as much courtesy and compassion as an adult does. In fact, she may be in even greater need of understanding and insight because she is at the mercy of others and relatively defenseless.

Perspective taking can be examined in two ways: gaining perspective on people and gaining perspective on problems. Let's inspect the skill in these two ways.

PERSPECTIVE ON PEOPLE

"In conflict situations there are often perceptual distortions concerning your own and the other person's behavior, motivations, and position."[2] Since we are in danger of perceiving ourselves and others incorrectly, how can we avoid this trap? What practical strategy can we use in our approach to problems and conflicts?

We can gain perspective on people through thinking logically. This is not to say that we can always understand others logically. People often behave in illogical ways, though it may make sense to them. We have no assurance that we can know why someone responds as he does. But we can attempt to use common sense in perceiving others' motives and behavior.

How do I do this? Where do I begin?

I begin by setting aside time to think about the person. I ask myself, "What do I know about this person? What do I know about his background or past experiences that color his interpretation of life?" Here is a true example. I know a man who has had difficulty relating to other people on the job. He would get upset if he thought he was not getting fair treatment. His actions indicated that he was insecure. I decided to get to know him better and discovered that he had grown up in foster homes, being moved from one family to another. Through these experiences he became insecure and adopted outward behaviors to hide his insecurity. The more I learned about him, the more I could understand why he reacted as he did. These insights were invaluable in problem-solving situations I faced with him.

When you face a problem with another person, use the following exercise. Sit down with paper and a pencil and begin to list what you know about the person. Separate facts from opinions. What do these facts tell you about this individual? What additional information do you need that would help you understand his behavior? Who might know the person better than you do who could help you understand this individual? What experiences have shaped his life and how he interprets the problem we face?

Your search must be undertaken to develop compassionate understanding, not as a means to manipulate, judge, or "win." When your approach is positive, it will begin to spill over into your relationship. Often, the other person will sense your genuine concern and will become more cooperative, more open to you.

Observe the other person. The writer of Proverbs observed

that "a happy heart makes the face cheerful, but heartache crushes the spirit."[3] He understood that a person's inner state is often revealed by facial expression, body posture, and other mannerisms. We can develop skill in observing people and the visual clues they give us. Sometimes merely reflecting our observations back to them is an invitation to talk about deeper issues that they are struggling with.

As we work with others in problem or conflict situations, we can be aware of visual "triggering behaviors" which they may display.

> *Awareness* of which behaviors are likely to start a needless conflict between you and others can help you eliminate many confrontations. Certain words, looks, or actions tend to "trigger" specific people into conflict. Often these triggering behaviors have little or nothing to do with present relationships. They may be rooted in early childhood experiences.[4]

By careful observation we can learn to pick up these triggering behaviors and know how to respond to them in a constructive way. They are like advance signals that caution us of coming conflicts.

We can become perceptive listeners. As you and I talk, we communicate not only factual information, but also attitudes, values, and emotions. Unfortunately, most people are poor listeners and completely miss verbal clues that help us understand the other person's perspective. Sometimes, subconscious motives and emotions push their way to the surface of the speaker's life and express themselves in subtle, verbal ways. The writer of Proverbs counseled that "the purposes of a man's heart are deep waters, but a man of understanding draws them out."[5]

I use the word "perceptive" deliberately when speaking of the act of listening. I use it to indicate an empathetic quality whereby the listener endeavors to "get inside the speaker's skin" to see what the speaker sees, feel what the speaker feels, discern what the speaker discerns.

The goal of listening is to understand the *content* of the other person's ideas or proposals, the *meaning* it has for him, and the *feelings* he has about it. That means being able to step into the other person's shoes and *view from his point of view* the things he is talking about.[6]

We can gain insight into others through prayer. Through prayer the Spirit of God is able to communicate wisdom and discernment to the child of God. I am not speaking of a casual approach to prayer. Rather, I mean a spirit of humility in which I come before the Lord with a sincere desire to receive insight into the needs, concerns, and the perspective of another. I must have a willingness to learn from the Lord and a willingness to act upon what He communicates to me. It is not an effort to get God on my side; it is an effort to know the mind of the Spirit.

PERSPECTIVE ON THE PROBLEM

We can apply our perspective-taking skill not only to people, but also to the problem itself. In fact, failing at this point may hinder us greatly because we will try to solve the problem without ample facts to come to the best solution.

I find it invaluable to ask myself several questions that help me gain perspective on the problem. First I ask, "How does the problem look through others' eyes? How do they perceive it?" Asking this question forces me to recognize that others have a perspective that I do not have. If I am honest, I admit that my understanding is limited and I need to see the problem in a larger context. In the book *Joining Together,* the authors underscore the importance of understanding the other person's perspective when dealing with conflicts.

Conflicts cannot be resolved if negotiators do not understand what they are disagreeing about. Only if you understand the differences between your position and your opponent's will you be able to propose potential agreements that may be acceptable to both parties. The general rule for negotiating conflicts of interest is to differentiate, then try to integrate your position and your opponent's. [7]

I also like to ask myself, "What do others have to gain or lose in this situation? What is important to them that is not important to me?" These questions challenge me to see that others may have motivations I do not have that will cause them to act in ways foreign to me. My solution might cause anxiety or fear because it jeopardizes their security, or costs them something of which I am not aware.

I find value in asking myself, "What facts am I overlooking?" Merely asking the question does not give me the facts, but it does tend to make me search for information I have overlooked.

The discipline of looking at the problem from a different perspective pays solid dividends. Many years ago I faced a baffling problem. I had an aggressive dog who put his front paws on the screen door and tore the screen. I could not solve my dilemma. One day I stood in the backyard and thought of all the possible ways the problem could be dealt with (including getting rid of the dog!). I let my mind go wild, considering any idea that occurred to me. Suddenly I knew what solution would work and be simple to apply. I built a ledge on the screen door so that the dog's feet rested on the ledge, rather than the screen. My point is that until I opened myself to consider facts I had overlooked or possible solutions I'd not considered, I was not in touch with all the insight I needed.

I have shared some questions that I ask myself to gain perspective. It is equally valuable to ask questions of other people. Don't limit your information seeking to those directly involved with the problem. I have found that one of the best ways to practice the perspective-taking skill is to seek information wherever I can find it. When I face a problem, I begin to ask questions of anyone who can enrich my perspective. I have never failed to gather fresh facts and insights that have been invaluable to me.

Before finishing this chapter, I would like to speak to one important issue. For many years I have been involved in pastoral counseling. One truth has stood out repeatedly as I have listened to individuals describe their interpersonal conflicts. Again and again I hear individuals describe the other person as mean, uncaring, and thoughtless. Yet, as I hear the other person and see the facts, I find the person making the accusations has formed a faulty perspective that intensified the conflict. *One of the major roadblocks to problem solving and conflict resolution is the tendency to impute evil motives and actions to others.* This tendency to attack, discredit, and suspect the other person is one of the most destructive behaviors I observe. All of us need to guard against it.

As with any skill development, this skill will take time to master; however, any effort you expend to increase your expertise in the perspective-taking skill will reward you handsomely. Learning to see issues from other people's point of view has enriched my life immeasurably and assisted me in facing problems with others. It pays big dividends.

Personal Discovery

1. The Bible counsels us to practice perspective taking. Look up the following verses and write in your own words what they tell you about this important skill.
   A. Proverbs 12:15
   B. Proverbs 20:5
   C. Romans 14:5–8
   D. Philippians 2:3,4

2. This chapter challenges you to understand the other person's point of view. Read the following statements.

Then visualize situations you have been in where these kinds of thoughts have occurred.

A. When I tell about my past, it's "meaningful sharing"; when you do it, you're egotistical.

B. When I sleep in late, it's because I need extra sleep; when you sleep in, it's because you're lazy.

C. When I take my time, it's because I want to do a quality job; when you do it, it's because you're "goofing off."

D. When I leave food on my plate, it's because I'm exercising discipline; when you do it, it's because you're wasteful.

E. When I act without being told, it's because I'm being responsible; when you do it, you're trying to impress the boss.

F. When I score 25 points in basketball, it's because I'm skillful; when you do it, you're showing off.

3. Make a list of people with whom you most often have misunderstandings. Include friends, neighbors, employers, relatives, business associates or co-workers, teachers, and others. Beside each name write what you think their perspective is in the misunderstanding between the two of you. Then answer these questions: (1) How can understanding their perspective be helpful in resolving differences? (2) How could your determination to understand their position or circumstances communicate love? (3) What information might you be failing to recognize that is important to the other person?

Personal Feedback

1. Practice your perspective-taking skill together. Take turns reading the following statements and then describe the potential thoughts and feelings a person in that situation might have.

What is it like if:

You must go to a class that you are failing and the teacher dislikes you?

You have a master's degree but are confined at home with two preschool children?

You are concerned about the quality of your work while your supervisor pushes for quantity?

You are a Sunday school teacher who loves children and wants to serve, but have a class that you are unable to control?

You are a junior higher who must move to a new state and attend a new school?

You are a full-time college student who must also work full-time to meet financial needs?

You are a single parent of three children and must work ten hours a day to meet financial needs?

You are going through a divorce?

You are eighty years old, hard of hearing, and live alone?

2. Describe to each other one situation in which you feel misunderstood. Talk about strategies to help others understand your perspective.

3. Describe a problem or conflict situation that has not been resolved. Let another person ask you the questions I've suggested under the Perspective on the Problem section of this chapter.

Chapter Sixteen

COMMUNICATION SKILLS

Have you ever found yourself in a potentially explosive situation? If you said the wrong word, someone would blow up, so you felt tension about what to say, wondering how the other person would react.

Jesus encountered such a situation during his earthly ministry. One hot, dusty day He rested beside a well on His journey from Judea to Galilee. As He sat there, he observed a Samaritan woman trudge down the path carrying an empty water container. He knew the burning thirst that cried out for fulfillment within her. He also understood the sensitive spirit she would have toward Him, a man and a Jew. She would watch every movement carefully; she would screen every word He spoke. If He wanted to address her problem, He would have to speak with wisdom and compassion.

The conversation that followed changed her life. Something occurred within her that she had never experienced before; something was awakened that touched her deeply. She tasted something that began to satisfy an intense thirst. Her own words give us a clue to the inner transformation that was beginning. When she returned to her village, her first words to her neighbors were "Come, see a man who told me everything I ever did. Could this be the Christ?"[1]

The entire event centered around a brief conversation that Jesus had with this lady. The dialogue recorded in John 4 could have occurred in five minutes, yet in that short time she was touched deeply. She experienced something she would never forget; she met someone she would always remember.

A few years ago I received a letter from a young man living in New Jersey. We had had a brief encounter, perhaps five years earlier, when he had visited relatives in the town where I lived. I only recall one conversation with this man (he was a teenager at the time of our conversation). The contents of the letter centered around that brief interchange. He said that I had encouraged him not to lose sight of God's faithfulness when times were difficult.

"Sometimes I'd get discouraged and be tempted to quit," he said. "Then I'd remember your words and would again look to Christ."

He described the stability and maturity God had built into his life. A God-centered perspective was a strong factor in the success he had experienced. He thanked me for my strategic input in his life.

Can you imagine my feelings as I laid the letter aside? I was amazed; I felt overwhelmed. God allowed me to experience that event as a quiet witness to the significance of brief encounters. Since that time, many other affirmations have occurred. I see consistent evidence of the power of our communication.

THE POWER OF EFFECTIVE COMMUNICATION

Words are powerful; listening is powerful. Each has potential to facilitate change in others; each has potential to inspire hope, insight, compassion. *But,* each also has potential to tear down, destroy, ruin.

Our communication is a clue to our maturity. One of Jesus' disciples said, "We all stumble in many ways. If anyone is never at fault in what he says, he is a perfect man, able to keep his whole body in check."[2] What issues from our mouth is an indication of what lies within us.

Our communication has the power to speak not only to

one's mind, but also to one's heart. It can touch emotions. "Pleasant words are a honeycomb, sweet to the soul and healing to the bones."[3] We come away from conversations not only intellectually, but emotionally stimulated from the interchange.

WHEN COMMUNICATION BREAKS DOWN

It would be tempting to speak only of the positive power of communication, but that would be dishonest. Communication has both positive and negative power. It can as easily tear down relationships as build them up. It can lead us to defeat as well as success.

> Eighty percent of the people who fail at work do so for one reason: they do not relate well to other people. One's productivity as a supervisor or manager, nurse or secretary, mental health worker or janitor, laborer, attorney, physician, clerk, or minister is greatly enhanced by the ability to communicate well. In fact, it is difficult to think of a single job in which communication is unimportant.[4]

What will defective or absent communication do to our relationships? What will it do to problem solving?

Ineffective communication destroys the potential for a quality relationship and opens the door for misunderstanding and hurt. It creates an unhealthy situation in which infection can set in, poisoning relationships.

Ineffective communication jeopardizes the exchange of resources. In problem solving we are exchanging ideas and insights. When communication breaks down, this process cannot continue efficiently. Resources you need are locked in my mind, unavailable to you; I am denied your insights. If interaction does occur through ineffective communication, what is transmitted will likely be distorted, so that we receive defective materials for the problem-solving process.

Ineffective communication also restricts the joy of mutual support and cooperative teamwork. Teamwork will be inefficient, leading to much struggle and confusion. The energy expended will seem not worth the benefits received. Our teamwork will be far less productive than it could be under positive circumstances.

Where ineffective communication exists, the opportunity to find healing, if the relationship has been damaged, cannot occur. In many instances, ineffective communication will lead to broken communication. Our opportunity to resolve differences is gone, but the problem remains, painfully reminding us of our brokenness. The positive memories remind us of what was, but the negative memories remind us of what now is.

I have not overstated the issue. Defective communication has ruined thousands of relationships between earnest people. Very seldom do "wicked" people come for marital counseling; rather, we find intelligent, responsible individuals who are trapped in misguided, inaccurate, negative communication patterns that follow a destructive cycle. The end product is pain, distance, and frequently, divorce. This same pattern can be observed in employer-employee, parent-child, neighbor-neighbor relationships.

WHEN MINDS DON'T MEET

Jesse Nirenberg suggests that there are five reasons why we have trouble getting through to others. [5] He believes that we have human tendencies that make it difficult to experience a meeting of our minds.

Nirenberg reminds us that we usually are *resistant to change*. We are not quick to receive new ideas that are significantly different from our own, especially when the new ideas or proposals threaten our security. We are more comfortable with our routines and habit patterns that feel comfortable and safe.

We also have the tendency to *center on our own thoughts rather than listen to others' thoughts*. When others are talking, we have our own thoughts to contend with. When they speak, we don't turn off our minds; rather, we continue a mental dialogue that interferes with perceptive listening. This "selective listening" causes problems because we do not hear the full message.

Humans also have the tendency to *practice wishful hearing*. We hear what we want to hear; we read into others' messages what we want them to say. This practice causes us to distort facts to fit our perception and wishes. "Wishful hearing in everyday affairs gives an angry or cheerful tone to a neutral voice. It supplies words that were never meant to be there, and gives meaning that originates only in the listener's mind."[6]

We all have the tendency to *make unwarranted assumptions*. We assume that others mean what they do not mean; we assume that others know what we are assuming. Consequently, we do not make our assumptions clear. The result is confusion and misunderstanding. We make false assumptions because we do not practice perspective-taking skills, seeing problems as others do.

Our fifth tendency is to *practice habitual secretiveness*. Many of us have been taught a sense of personal privacy that carries over into our communication. We keep ideas and information to ourselves; we want to retain our private information. Then we proudly feel that we are more knowledgeable than others. This tendency defeats us when others need to share the information for mutual problem solving. In the end, we cheat ourselves, as well as others.

If we are to become skilled problem solvers, we must find ways to overcome these five enemies that attack a meeting of our minds. Effective problem solving demands that we share the mental resources within each of us. Only then will we have full resources available to all involved to work together for the best solution. Each of us individually must develop skill at facing and overcoming the tendencies that defeat us.

BUILDING COMMUNICATION SKILLS

Thus far we have been exploring the incredible potential of effective communication. We have seen how resistant we are to achieving harmony of thinking. So to excel in problem solving, we must take seriously the challenge to build sound communication skills. Let's consider the following questions: How do we build effective communication skills? How do I go about it?

I would like to pursue these questions by identifying several practical ways we can enrich our communication. Communication is a complex process, but certain basic issues will give us a fundamental grasp of the process. In this chapter, I have tried to extract the critical dimensions of communication skills and explore them.

First, the effective communicator *chooses a productive style.* I find two styles of communication identified in Ephesians 4:29. Paul counseled the Ephesians, "Do not let any unwholesome talk come out of your mouths, but only what is helpful for building others up according to their needs, that it may benefit those who listen." First, he described what I call STYLE 2. STYLE 2 communication is negative and exists when there is communication characterized by

BLAMING
YELLING
DEMANDING
COMMANDING
SARCASM
THREATENING
INTERROGATING
IGNORING

STYLE 2 is *not* an effective way to solve problems; it is a very effective way to escalate problems into conflicts. The person who resorts to this approach condemns himself or herself to strained, broken relationships, and conflict. No healthy person wants to be related to by a STYLE 2 approach to communication.

The Bible is very blunt about this. We read, "With his mouth the godless destroys his neighbor" and "A man who lacks judgment derides his neighbor."[7] This is a straightforward way to call us to responsibility in our communication. Although STYLE 2 communication is destructive, many individuals, including Christians, commonly use this approach to relate to others.

Ephesians 4:29 indicates the approach we are called to use, to become proficient in. I call it STYLE 1 communication. This approach is characterized by talk that "is helpful for building others up according to their needs." STYLE 1 communication is characterized by

HONESTY
AFFIRMATION
EMPATHETIC LISTENING
SUPPORTIVE COMMENTS
SHARED EXPERIENCE
ENCOURAGEMENT
FRIENDSHIP

Notice the impact of STYLE 1 communication on the hearer: It builds the hearer up and is constructive, positive, helpful. STYLE 1 is oriented toward solving problems, not creating conflict, and is based on the attitude of respect and good will. Where differences and misunderstandings have occurred, this approach brings healing. The Bible says that "reckless words pierce like a sword, but the tongue of the wise brings healing."[8]

Many of us have been taught an approach to problem solving that is hard-nosed, win-lose, antagonistic. I say without question, this is unbiblical. It leads to strife, hostility, and hurt. As people called to redemptive relationships, we cannot accept an approach that is not based upon love and seeking another's well-being.

STYLE 1 communication—communication that is compassionate, respectful and affirming—does not overlook negative situations. *We can always deal with negative situations with a positive attitude.* Just because someone treats us harshly does not mean that we must resort to threats, blame, or yelling. We are more effective in coping with problem situations, even disobedience, with STYLE 1 communication.

I have been committed to practicing STYLE 1 communication for many years. I have found it far more effective, far more constructive, far more supportive of relationships, far more productive to problem solving than STYLE 2. Yet, I consistently observe well-educated adults using STYLE 2 tactics and creating havoc in relationships, since it inevitably fosters conflict.

Our communication is a means of grace; that is, it is one of the means God chooses to minister His love to others. Once this mighty truth is comprehended, we realize how significant our communication can become. What our mouth speaks has the potential to bless someone in the name of the Lord. Or, our mouth can be a source of hurt and destruction.

What I have written may sound "spiritual" in a book concerning problem solving. Actually, that's just the point. *Effective problem solving is the proper application of spiritual reality.* When I speak as the Spirit of God is prompting me to speak, it will bring significant blessing to my approach to problem solving.

Second, in effective problem solving *we state our intentions at the beginning.* Individuals come to problem situations with years of past experience. Many of these experiences have not been pleasant. People learn to be suspicious about how others relate to them. A friend of mine once said something like this: "In my business I am often invited out to lunch by a salesman. I know that he is taking me to lunch because he hopes to gain something from me from the time. He wants to make a sale. It has caused me to wonder how many times people have treated me kindly because they want something from me." My friend reveals a trait many of us have developed: We are suspicious about the motives of others as they relate to us.

Since others do not know our motives, it is essential that we clarify them, especially in problem-solving or conflict situations. At the beginning of our interaction, a simple statement of "My intention is . . . " will clue others in to what we are trying to achieve.

When Winnie and I were first married, I had unrealistic expectations about the care of our house. I'd become frustrated when every item was not in its proper place. This would be followed by STYLE 2 communication, which was dehumanizing to Winnie. In time she became sensitive to my criticism about her housekeeping. Finally, I realized the foolishness of my way and began to change my behavior. But by then Winnie was sensitive to any action I would make toward housekeeping. If I began to pick up newspapers or other articles in the living room, she would get upset, thinking I was angry with her. I realized that I needed to state my intentions *at the beginning of my actions*. I'd say something like, "I'm not irritated at you; I just want to pitch in and help." As I consistently did this, my wife began to see my actions in a new light and the tension related to care of the house diminished. This simple statement has helped us diffuse many potential conflict issues because it has communicated our positive, healthy intentions to each other.

When you face problem or conflict issues, learn to state your intentions.

> "I'm not angry that you bought the dress; I'm just curious why you wanted it."

"My intention is not to criticize the way you did it; I want to let you know that a new technique has been developed that reduces the time involved."

"I'm not mad that you got a 'C' (my intentions are not to express anger); "I'm wondering if you need more assistance."

Many people do not realize that others frequently *misinterpret our good intentions*. Consequently, we must become skillful at introducing our intentions wisely to help others see them. Only then will our good accomplish good.

Let's move to a third area of skill development. To communicate effectively *we learn to speak wisely*. Problem solving is a process that requires precision. Nowhere will the precision pay richer dividends than in our communication. We cannot afford to be sloppy in our communication skills.

We can practice wise communication in several ways. For one thing, we can learn to distinguish facts from opinions. In problem solving we should major on facts. I am not saying that we never express opinions; however, when we express opinions, we should realize that that is what they are: opinions. Many problem–solving situations become little more than pooled ignorance, rather than a serious pursuit of truth. Individuals are airing opinions that contribute little to finding an excellent solution.

Another way we practice wise communication is by being wise in our choice of words. The Bible reminds us that "the lips of the righteous know what is fitting."[9] Skillful communication requires precision and discipline to avoid unrestrained venting of emotions, thoughtless rambling, and insignificant opinions. The skilled communicator harnesses his resources and uses them wisely to accomplish the task. Notice how the writer of Proverbs stressed this point:

"He who guards his lips guards his soul, but he who speaks rashly will come to ruin."[10]

"He who guards his mouth and his tongue keeps himself
from calamity."[11]

The skilled communicator will exercise caution in the use
of inappropriate humor in problem or conflict situations.
Often sarcasm is masked behind humor and others perceive
it as a put-down. When someone is grappling with a
problem that has personal implications, he does not appreciate others taking it lightly or making comic remarks.

We can develop our communication skills in a fourth way.
We give and receive feedback. Feedback is telling others what
we see or hear to help them see themselves through the eyes
of another person. It is invaluable to problem solving.
Consider what the following feedback accomplishes.

"As I listen to you, your voice sounds tense. Are you
feeling upset?"

"You said 'Twenty dollars.' I think you meant twenty
cents."

"Your last comment was very helpful to me. I can see
why you wanted to do it your way."

Giving feedback not only clarifies information to the one
receiving it, it also communicates a commitment to listen
and a respect for what the other person is saying. It expresses
a positive attitude toward problem solving.

Anyone who takes communication seriously realizes how
easy it is to be misunderstood. Such a person will want
others to give feedback to know if he is being accurately
understood. Though it is not always pleasant to hear others'
honest perception of us and what we are saying, we need to
receive it.

The fifth area of communication skill development is
crucial to productive problem solving. *We learn to be a
perceptive listener.* Listening is one half of the communication
process. What a vital part it is! Unfortunately few people are
perceptive listeners, and it is one of the most practical ways
to communicate love.

The following suggestions are beginning steps to increase your listening skills. For a fuller treatment of the subject, I would recommend that you read the book *Listening: The Christian's Guide to Loving Relationships.*[12]

1. Discover when you are a poor listener (when you are tired, when you are emotionally upset, when you want to express your ideas) and learn how to deal with it.
2. Learn to listen for emotions, as well as ideas. Consider emotions as a "second language" the person is using.
3. Recognize that others use the same words with different meanings. Learn to ask questions to discover what the other person means. Ask, "Do you mean . . . ?"
4. Organize your own thoughts to know what to listen for. Ask yourself, "What information do I need from this person?" "What has been left unsaid?" "What is the problem like from his perspective?"
5. Recognize and remove your "listening filters." These are attitudes and biases that will influence how you listen and how you interpret what you hear.

I have said that listening is a critical aspect of problem solving. It is the primary means of tapping into the other person's resources to achieve the best solution. Effort you expend to develop your listening skills will be richly rewarded.

TO GROW OR NOT TO GROW

Humans are odd creatures! We expend enormous amounts of time and money to educate our young, yet we neglect to train them in some of the most essential skills. We teach communication skills in haphazard, ineffective ways. I know of no school that offers a class in communication to grade-school aged children. I was well into my adult years before I began to discover the basic principles of communication; nevertheless, these skills have enriched my life immeasurably. Recently I introduced a man in his sixties to communication skills that were invaluable to him in rebuilding his marriage. Later he said to me, "I'm seeing how valuable these are to all areas of my life. They are as appropriate for relating to people at work as they are for family members." It's a shame that he had to wait until so late in life to make this discovery.

Communication is a complex process; however, we can practice basic skills that will increase our effectiveness. These skills will reward us in every relationship. They will help us solve problems and avoid the danger of those problems degenerating into painful conflicts. When we build effective communication skills, we not only do ourselves a favor, but we also demonstrate to others the value we place on relationships.

Personal Discovery

1. Memorize Ephesians 4:29.

2. James 1:19 says that "everyone should be quick to listen, slow to speak, and slow to become angry." Apply this truth to your own problem-solving skills by completing the following statements.
   "When I am discussing a problem with _____, being quick to listen will help me because . . ."
   "When _____ and I are facing a problem, my being slow to speak will help because . . ."
   "If I am quick to listen and slow to speak, it might reduce the potential for either of us to get angry because . . ."

3. I have stressed the importance of listening. Evaluate your listening skills by responding to the following questions.

	Yes	Some-times	No
1. Do I know how to listen for emotions?			
2. Do I decide in advance what I am listening for?			
3. Do I listen in a way that allows the speaker to express his feelings?			
4. Do I decide whether I will listen for facts, opinions, or feelings?			
5. Can I sort out the points the speaker is making even if his speech is very emotional?			
6. Do I tend to block out what is said if I disagree with the speaker?			
7. Do I identify key points or words to help me remember the points the speaker made?			
8. Do I tend to be planning my response when I should be listening?			
9. Do I recognize situations in which I tend to be a poor listener, and know how to cope with them?			
10. Do I give the speaker my undivided attention?			
11. Do I use non-judgmental questions to help the speaker himself?			
12. Do I view listening as a way to encourage the speaker?			

Personal Feedback

1. I have shared Jesse Nirenberg's five reasons why minds often don't meet. Discuss together which of the five you are most likely to practice. Try to come up with a better strategy that will increase your communication skill.

2. This chapter describes a productive and a nonproductive style of communication (STYLE 1 and STYLE 2). Give each other specific feedback as to when you have observed either kind of behavior in the other person. If you are describing STYLE 2 behavior give a specific example of a more effective way of communicating. Remember, *a negative situation can always be dealt with using STYLE 1 communication.* Be cautious as you give feedback that you don't slip into STYLE 2 communication.

3. Discuss the following questions together.
   A. With whom do you have the most difficulty talking over problems? Why?
   B. What poor communication habits have you developed? What could be done about replacing these with more effective ones?
   C. Which of the skills described in this chapter do you consistently practice? Which ones need developing?

Chapter Seventeen
PROBLEM-IDENTIFICATION
SKILLS

The next two chapters focus on the problem-solving process. It is tempting to outline the process in one chapter, but after careful evaluation, I realize that too much needs to be discussed. I have chosen to divide the process into two shorter units to allow you opportunity to digest it. As you explore the concepts in these chapters, keep in mind that we are covering one process in two stages.

I have said I find it odd that we do not systematically teach our children how to become skilled problem solvers. They will face problems and conflicts all their lives. It would seem wise to give them the tools to make their work more efficient, more productive. Yet, it is rare to find a parent who is disciplined in problem solving and who passes the skills on to his children in a careful, practical manner.

In problem solving we attempt to do five things: 1. We assess where we are now. 2. We assess where we would like to be, or what we would like to see happen to improve our lives, relationships, or circumstances. 3. We try to discover the steps necessary to get us to this desired goal. 4. We begin acting to see it happen. 5. We periodically evaluate or monitor our progress and see if we need to make midcourse corrections to keep on target.

As we work through the problem-solving process, it is essential to keep three facts in mind. All that is described in the next two chapters rests on these foundation stones. Though I may not repeat them, please keep in mind that everything that is said is built upon these three principles. First, *a genuine, prayerful spirit must accompany each step of the problem-solving process.* I do not mean that we stop and pray every time we move to a new step. I mean that we have a true spirit of dependence on the Lord to oversee the process and actively seek His guidance.

Second, *problem solving is not an attempt to win over someone else.* Together we commit to seek a wise, productive solution from the Lord that is in His best interests. We believe God when He says, "I will instruct you and teach you in the way you should go; I will counsel you and watch over you."[1]

Third, *problem solving is a discipline.* Most of us are lazy when it comes to problem solving. We want to take the easy way out; we resist the rigors of a careful, orderly process that requires us to take precise steps in logical sequence. We'd rather "fly by the seat of our pants." No wonder the results are dissatisfying or ineffective.

To help you establish the discipline of effective problem solving, I am asking you to do the following things:

1. Set aside specific time to work on the problem.
2. Write out the process.
3. Do not take shortcuts. Follow the process as prescribed.

Later feel free to modify the process to fit your needs. For now, however, it is important that you experience the process as it is outlined here to establish orderly thought patterns. A disciplined way of thinking is an essential element of the problem-solving process.

With these preliminary issues before us, we can now move into stage one of the problem-solving process.

STAGE ONE: THE PROBLEM

We face a problem. Something doesn't fit; something blocks progress; someone doesn't agree with us on a course of action. What do we do? I am going to suggest three steps that will help us identify and better understand the problem that confronts us.

Step One: The Problem As I See It

Most people begin problem solving without a clear, accurate understanding of the problem. Often the perceived problem is not the real problem. All action that follows is wasted because it is exhausted on the wrong issue. Valuable energy is used up that is needed to attack the real problem.

To avoid this mistake, I suggest that you begin by stating the problem as you see it. *Write it down.* The act of writing helps you discipline your thought process. Seeing it in writing allows you to clarify your thinking. Focus first on the *cognitive aspects*—What are the facts or details of the problem as I see it? If the problem has various elements, try to identify them. Also, think through the context in which the problem occurs.

Bolton makes an excellent suggestion about defining the problem. He says, "For a win/win outcome, the problem is stated in terms of *needs—not solutions.*"[2] He has found that when people think of problems, they think in terms of solutions. The result is a greater tendency to be forced into a win/lose situation. By stating the problem in terms of needs, the focus of concern is "How can our needs be met?" rather than "Who will win?" or "Whose solution is best?"

Next, write down the *emotional aspects* of the problem as you see them: What are the emotional feelings I have toward the problem and toward those involved in the problem? Try to be as honest as you can about your feelings, even if you don't like them.

At the same time you are writing down your understanding of the cognitive and emotional aspects of the problem, others who are involved should do the same.

Step Two: The Problem As You See It

We tend to forget this step. We focus our concern on the problem as we see it and fail to consider how the problem looks from the other person's perspective. Remember that one of the key skills you are trying to develop is perspective taking. Step two forces us to look at the problem as others see it.

Use the same approach to write out this step. What are the cognitive aspects of the problem for others? State the problem in terms of their needs. Jot down the emotions others are experiencing, or will experience.

Many problems are never solved in an effective way because we lack the data known only to others. Look at this example from Art Linkletter's life.

When Art Linkletter arrived at an airport in Jordan to make a TV Christmas special, a high-ranking Arab official told him he wouldn't be allowed to take pictures there. Keeping calm (although he had a written contract to do the filming), Linkletter asked why the permit was revoked. The Arabs, it seemed, were upset because twice as much film had been shipped to Israel as to Jordan. They assumed this meant the special would be biased in Israel's favor.

This wasn't the case. More film was needed in Israel because inside shots were filmed there, and this took more film. But rather than arguing this point with the Arab official, Linkletter said, "Maybe I don't understand all the available opportunities for pictures. Do you have a map that shows each place having to do with Christ?"

The official proudly showed him the many sites on the map; Linkletter promised to give equal coverage; and the difficulty was settled.

Whenever you're tempted to argue strenuously with someone who says "no," stop for a minute. Perhaps Linkletter's thoughtful "Maybe I don't understand" would help you reach a quicker agreement and avoid needless hassling. After all, perhaps you *don't* understand what the other person's objections are. In any case, learning the cause of the problem may help you clear it up.[3]

Step Three: The Problem As We See It

Steps one and two are completed by yourself; others involved in the process are doing the same. In step three everyone comes together to begin the mutual process of working toward an agreement about what the problem is. Up to this point we have carefully identified our own thoughts and perceptions about the problem. Now we begin to check out our insights and perceptions with those of others.

Many of us make a common error: We assume others see the problem as we do. This is seldom true. Certain facts will be available to you that are not available to me. You will perceive facts and circumstances through different filters than I will. Step three brings us together to compare information and perceptions.

I would suggest that you share information around the three themes I have indicated: cognitive details, the problem in terms of need, and emotional aspects of the problem. Though it may seem to be a nuisance, *write out your common understandings*. This strengthens understanding and reduces the potential for unstated assumptions, perceptions, and misunderstandings.

I have emphasized the importance of clarifying needs as essential to seeking a solution or solutions. In step three we write a mutually understood statement of the problem in terms of need, either common to all involved or individual. Here are some suggestions to help you.

1. Distinguish between means and end. What you state as a need may really be a *means* to achieve a need. Suppose you and another family member want to watch two different programs on TV. Each may say, "I *need* the

TV!" Maybe not. Careful diagnosis may reveal that one person is bored and has need for meaningful activity; the other wants to listen to a news broadcast to keep up on current events. Several solutions may be acceptable to meet each need: A variety of activities might alleviate the boredom; the news can be heard on the radio.

2. Complete the statement "I need . . ." Then discuss whether this is the real need or a *means* to achieve the need. For example, look at the "I need" statements below and ask if they state a need, or a means to meet a need.
   "I need the car tonight."
   "I need you to stay home tonight."
   "I need to go to a restaurant."
   "I need a raise."
   Each is a means to achieve something else: transportation, companionship, food, money.

3. Practice perceptive listening when others identify their problems. Ask yourself, "Is he talking about the real need?" Try to raise questions that will help the person identify the real need.

One remaining issue needs to be addressed. In identifying the problem that is confronting us, we may add too many unrelated details that will be excess baggage. Be cautious about "compounding" the problem. We can compound the problem in a variety of ways.

We can intellectually compound: We add details that are peripheral to the real issue. I suggest that in step one you begin by writing down the facts as freely as possible. Then determine what the critical issues are. Try to hone the issues down to the basic information needed. The same process occurs in step three. We begin by getting all the information before us. Then, we distill it until we have the essential data that we can work with.

We can emotionally compound: We allow unnecessary emotions to accumulate that are not really helpful to the process. Sometimes these can be dealt with prior to coming to the problem. I may spend time clarifying my feelings, resolving those that will be detrimental. At other times emotions can be processed during step one or step three. In fact, we may not be aware of them until we are analyzing the dynamics of the problem.

We can socially compound: We engage in "socializing," "shooting the breeze," rather than focusing our attention on the problem at hand. In the process we clutter our minds with unnecessary details that hinder clear, accurate perception. Social compounding may result from an individual's nervousness about the problem, or it may be based on poor problem-solving habits.

We can spiritually compound: We spiritualize issues needlessly. We demand theological defense of people's ideas or opinions when it will add nothing significant to the problem-solving process. I am not suggesting that we leave our values and commitment out of problem solving; I am saying that often a *needless* spiritualizing of problems causes distraction, confusion, and harm.

WHEN AND WHERE?

I realize that the process I am outlining here may appear elaborate. You might ask, "Are you suggesting that I approach every problem situation with this complete approach? Should I write out *every* problem in this way?"

No!

But you should keep two guidelines in mind. First, in learning these skills you need to subject yourself to the discipline of practice. It would be wise to go through the process with smaller, less intense problems as a means of mastering the skill. Then when you encounter more serious problems, you will have gained proficiency. I have spoken of the danger of "flying by the seat of your pants," approaching problem solving with no carefully tested, effective plan. I am asking you to go through that discipline.

Second, as you practice the skills, they become a way of thinking. As you practice defining problems in terms of needs, you begin to think that way automatically. You may begin to see that you no longer need to write problems out, because your thought processes are doing that for you.

Third, you will want to follow this approach carefully with problems that are complex, emotionally powerful, have serious consequences, or resist solutions. You may find it helpful to list problems that have been defeating you for some time, or ones that are harmful to your relationships with others.

Personal Discovery

1. Success in problem solving comes through healthy attitudes and effective skills. In this chapter I am saying that a person needs to discipline himself to learn the problem-solving process. Perhaps this is a good time to ask yourself if you are satisfied merely reading this book, or if you want to master the disciplines. Will you really gain what you need in actual problem-solving situations you now face if you don't begin to work through the process described in this chapter? Do you need to *write down* your problem/conflict and think it through on paper to gain the skill that will benefit you for the remainder of your life?

2. Determining the needs of individuals is essential to interpersonal problem solving. To help you personalize this truth, work through the following practice exercise.

Read each of the statements and try to determine what the person's *real* need is. Also ask yourself if this would be the best means to meet the need. Then try to identify other ways the need could be met. Write your observations next to each statement.

"I need a different job."

"You need to be quiet."

"Leave me alone!"

"I need new clothes."

"I hate this kitchen!"

"School is boring."

"You need to be home by six o'clock tonight."

"I need to use the phone."

3. People often express their needs in conversation, but we may not notice or misunderstand them. The following list suggests needy people. Beside each person write down what his specific need is, then jot down several examples of statements the person might make in an attempt to have his need understood. Include statements that might be misunderstood by others.

An employer who is frustrated that his employees are coming to work late.

A lonely person.

A teenager who wants to stay out past curfew.

A spouse who feels neglected.

A child who is afraid of the dark.

A parent who sees his child
making unwise choices.

4. Think through the following questions related to your
   own life.
   A. How do you communicate your needs to others?
   B. How skilled are you at discerning your own and
      others' needs in problem and conflict situations you
      face? Can you think of incidents when your perceived
      needs were not your real needs? Can you identify
      situations in which someone misunderstood your
      needs and it led to conflict?
   C. How skilled are you at recognizing both the cogni-
      tive and emotional aspects of problems in yourself?
      In others?

Personal Feedback

1. Each person should write down one real or fictional
   problem. If the problem is real, do not include the actual
   names of the persons involved. Keep the problem
   statements brief. Have each person read his problem
   aloud. Then try to identify the following information.
   A. What is the real need? (There may be more than one.)
   B. What are potential emotions that may arise in this
      situation?
   C. What are some possible ways the need could be met?

2. Discuss the issue of intellectually, emotionally, socially,
   and spiritually compounding problems. Try to give examples of each of these from your own experience.

Chapter Eighteen
SOLUTION-SEEKING SKILLS

Chapter seventeen focused on the *problem*. How do we identify it? How do we know that the perceived problem is the real problem? How do we identify the problem in terms of need, rather than solution?

In this chapter, I discuss the remaining steps in the problem-solving process that will lead us to the best solution. Since this chapter is a continuation of the process begun in the earlier chapter, keep in mind that the steps outlined here are built upon the previous ones.

Step Four: Generating Potential Solutions

At this point we have identified the problem. Together we have stated it in terms of a need, or needs, we have. Now we are ready to search out solutions that will adequately meet these needs.

Many people make a mistake here. They start looking for *the* solution. Rather than thinking divergently—"What are all the possible solutions," they think convergently—"What is the solution to this problem?" Immediately they limit themselves by considering the one answer instead of all the creative options.

Step Four calls us to *brainstorm*, a simple technique in which we generate as many solutions as possible. To brainstorm, some basic rules must be followed.

1. Work for quantity of solutions, not quality of solutions.

By emphasizing quantity, we exhaust the common solutions and then are challenged to think of new, novel approaches. Having a quantity of solutions gives us more raw material to develop a quality solution later in the process. I am not suggesting that we don't want quality solutions; what I am saying is that we don't evaluate at this stage. By getting a quantity of potential solutions we have more resource to work with to get the quality that we want. Quality is the concern of step five and step six.

2. No evaluation. If someone suggests a potential solution, no one decides whether it is good or bad, whether it will work or not, whether it has weaknesses or not. At the brainstorming phase these responses are not appropriate. They inhibit the free flow of ideas. When we begin to evaluate, we reject ideas too prematurely. Brainstorming actually encourages "wild ideas." Later we will have opportunity to evaluate our potential solution; now we want to be certain that we leave nothing out.

3. "Hitchhike!" Hitchhiking is building on someone else's thoughts. Let others' ideas stimulate your mind to generate other possibilities. Try to modify what someone else has suggested—add new features or change the order.

One sure way to improve your capacity to generate solutions is to learn to ask yourself questions. To develop this practice, you may want to keep a list before you to coach your mind. Here are some starters.

How could the situation be changed?

How have other people done it differently?

How could I change or adapt to accomplish it?

What could I add to it? Take away? Reverse?

Who are the people that are involved? What are their resources?

What other resources are available that I've overlooked?

Where has this same thing happened in a different context?

What could be substituted?

What would happen if we waited? Never did anything?

What am I leaving out? Whom am I leaving out? What
have I overlooked?

Remember, write your ideas down. You are gathering
ideas to use in seeking the best possible solution. You need
the ideas in front of you. If you try to keep them in your
mind, you will forget them. Write them down.

Step Five: Evaluating Potential Solutions

We have a list of solution ideas before us. We have
exhausted our minds to generate as much data as possible.
Now, what do we do with it?

First, keep in mind that we may need more than one
solution. When we defined the problem in terms of needs,
we opened ourselves to the possibility that individual needs
may require different solutions.

Second, submit the potential solutions to questions that
will help you evaluate them. Consider these.

What are the strengths of this solution?

What are its weaknesses?

What will be the consequences for us if this solution is
chosen? For others?

What will this solution accomplish?

Third, consider combining proposed solutions to
strengthen them. This may entail taking elements from one
solution and adding them to another. Don't hesitate to work
with your list of solutions to find the best possible answer
for the needs you have defined.

Step Six: Deciding on the Best Solution

Now you are at the point of decision making. You have
analyzed your data thoroughly and must now make a
decision.

Be certain that you have not neglected the emotional

issues related to the problem. Some individuals are less sensitive to emotional needs in others and feel that caring for the cognitive aspects of the problem is enough. I recall counseling with a couple concerning a marital problem. One spouse had indicated strong feelings related to the difficulty. After a period of interaction the other person said, "Well, now we've talked about this, and each of us understands the other. I guess we've finished." The partner responded, "No way! I've still got emotions that I need to express before we're finished."

Several guidelines are helpful for decision making.

1. Be committed to achieve a *mutual agreement*. Determine that you will find consensus. Any approach that uses a win/lose strategy will be less effective. The win/lose approach tends to undermine trust, emphasize power, and reduce mutual motivation to implement the solution.

One of the best ways to approach decision making is to say to others involved, "Let's determine to find the solution that we all feel is honoring to God and will mutually meet our needs." This raises the decision-making process above our own interests and submits it to a higher goal.

Be careful about letting individuals defer the decision to others. This can be an avoidance tactic: "I don't want to share responsibility for the outcome." The decision should be mutually agreed on; the outworking of the solution is then the responsibility of all.

2. To avoid making the decision-making process unnecessarily complicated, begin by having each person identify the solution that he would most favor. Then have him list acceptable alternatives. This reduces the need to consider each solution that has been identified and builds a foundation for agreement. We know what others prefer and what they are willing to accept as alternate solutions.

It is also wise to help individuals consider whether they advocate a solution because of personal bias. Many of us will not recognize this fact unless we are challenged to consider it. If we understand that our decision is based on bias, we may be open to consider other options. When a warm, positive environment exists, the potential for honest communication allows these questions to be raised.

3. When faced with decision making, we are wise to consider: Who has the greatest investment in the problem? Who has the most to lose? Who will be responsible to implement the solution? Who will give time to it? Who will expend personal resources? These questions remind us that we all participate in the decision, but some carry more responsibility or feel more impact than others.

4. Consider the relationship between cost and benefit. What appears as a desirable solution may be expensive in terms of time, money, and energy. Some solutions may have higher risks and require more effort.

5. Be cautious about making decisions too quickly. It is also possible to procrastinate, but allow time for everyone to digest the issues and monitor their emotions. The next day many people have regretted a decision that was hastily made. I have a friend who counseled me never to make an expensive purchase on the same day I saw the item. I see the wisdom in his statement.

Once you have made the decision, you should consider writing it so all parties involved have a clear, visible agreement. This is especially important when the decision being made has significant implications. I have observed numerous incidents where verbal agreements were made, but later, people had different perceptions of the agreement. Many situations ended with conflict because the decisions had been committed to memory, and upon recall, each person's memory was different.

Step Seven: Acting On Our Decision

The decision has been agreed on, but we have not reached the end of the process yet. In fact, in a sense we are just beginning. We are just beginning to implement the solution, which may require more energy than the rest of the process. Thinking through the steps of implementation is essential. To do this, I suggest we ask ourselves a series of questions.

How will we proceed? What is the process we will need to follow? If we don't ask this question, we will not have any sense of direction or know what is entailed in working out the solution. We must plan the action steps that lead to the solution being realized.

While we are considering how we will proceed, it may be wise to consider: *When will we implement the solution?* This helps us consider the question of timing. Now may not be the best time to act on the decision. If not, when is best?

What obstacles will we face? What resistance will we encounter? What could go wrong? What will need special attention? These questions alert us to potential dangers, roadblocks, or forces that we may find along the route to success. Some cannot be anticipated; they will pop up unaware along the path. Others, however, can be foreseen, and plans can be made to cope with them when they occur.

What resources will be required? By the word "resources" I mean both people and things. Actually, this question should have been raised in step five, but it occurs here as a part of the administrative process necessary to implement the solution. Mobilizing key resources is one way to guarantee that we will achieve what we want to accomplish.

Who will be responsible for implementing the solution? Who will do the actual work? Sometimes we face situations in which an individual has been given responsibility for a task, but not given the authority to carry it out. In step six that issue needs to be clarified. The individual entrusted with the responsibility needs to know that others give him the authority to see that the problem is resolved. This will also mean that the person has to have freedom to make decisions.

Who will need to be informed of the decision? Decisions frequently impact people outside the decision-making group. Someone must accept responsibility to inform them of the decision. A common error in decision-making groups is neglecting to communicate essential information to others who will be affected. People resent having issues that affect them decided without their being informed of them. Wherever possible they should be kept informed from the beginning. If they have input, a channel should be provided to receive it. When the decision has been reached, they should be fully informed.

When and how will we evaluate the process and the outcome? This is another phase of problem solving that is sometimes omitted. When solutions are being worked out over a period of time, evaluation should occur during the process. This provides opportunity for "midcourse correction." If changes need to be made, this can be done at an appropriate time to allow the process to operate more efficiently.

Evaluation will need to occur at the completion of the process. This helps us learn from what has taken place and become more skilled in facing future problems. We gain experience from solving each problem.

If you ever had any doubts, you should be certain now that problem solving is WORK, especially when we are faced with hard issues. My goal in the past two chapters has been threefold. First, I want you to see that problem solving is a *process*. It is an exercise in moving from point A to point B to point C. I also want you to develop a plan that makes you effective as a problem solver. I have outlined such a plan with the hope that you will develop skill in problem solving. Finally, I want to give you a plan that will help you *think* clearly and effectively when you encounter problems. I said earlier that too many people stumble and bungle through problems without a disciplined plan. They reap the results of their approach.

I encourage you to practice the problem-solving process until you achieve a natural proficiency. I am outlining it in chart form below to encourage you to make your own copies and use it as a means of developing your skill.

PROBLEM-SOLVING PROCESS

Step One: Problem as I See It
  A. Problem defined as NEED
  B. Cognitive aspect (facts, details)
  C. Emotional aspect
Step Two: Problem as You See It
  A. Problem defined as NEED
  B. Cognitive aspect
  C. Emotional aspect
Step Three: Problem as We See It (We agree about)
  A. Problem agreement
  B. Cognitive agreement
  C. Emotional agreement
Step Four: Generating Potential Solutions
Step Five: Evaluating Potential Solutions
Step Six: Deciding on the Best Solution
Step Seven: Acting on the Decision

Personal Discovery

1. Brainstorming is an important skill for generating solutions to problems and a valuable skill to add to your problem-solving skills.

   I have posed several questions below that stimulate brainstorming. I would like you to select one per day for the next seven days and write down as many solutions as you can dream up, using the guidelines discussed in this chapter. After you have generated many ideas, review them and select one that you would like to implement. In the process *have fun*.

   A. List as many ways as you can to improve your personal Bible study. (Don't settle for less than ten new ideas.)
   B. List twenty-five ways you can communicate "I love you" to another person.

C. Jot down fifteen ways to improve your child's education. If you don't have a child, choose a niece, nephew, or grandchild.

D. Think up nineteen ways to improve your job or work environment.

E. Generate twenty-one ideas to increase your knowledge of a subject in which you are interested.

F. List twenty-six ways you can meet new people.

G. Brainstorm seventeen ways you can improve a current relationship.

2. Why not start your own plan to improve your skill in brainstorming? For the next thirty days brainstorm a new idea each day. Be sure to accept the discipline of writing down your idea and keep trying to generate a longer list. Remember, the new, novel ideas come after we have exhausted the common ones.

3. We may become skilled in generating solutions, but it is still essential to discover the best solution for us. This, too, requires precise, disciplined thinking.

Review the five guidelines I've suggested in this chapter for deciding on the solution to implement. Ask yourself, Am I presently using these guidelines in problem solving? If not, which ones do I need to begin practicing? It might be valuable to read over the guidelines prior to beginning the problem-solving process with someone else.

Personal Feedback

1. Brainstorming with others is a helpful way to stretch our thinking. To do this, gather several miscellaneous objects (hat, plate, broom). Have one person hold up the object and everyone think of new uses for these familiar objects.

Then think of how the object could be modified or adapted. Or, think of ways it could be improved. How could two objects together create a new object? Remember to follow the guidelines for brainstorming outlined in this chapter.

After the brainstorming activity discuss the following questions.

A. How can an activity such as this improve our ability to brainstorm in actual problem situations?

B. What are some guidelines for evaluating solutions in problem situations?

C. What are other brainstorming activities that we could use to improve our thinking?

2. How we implement decisions is as important as how we make them. Discuss the following questions to think through this aspect of problem solving.

A. Are you more skilled in thinking up solutions or in putting them into practice?

B. How difficult is it for you to implement decisions when you have to work with others?

C. Which of the questions under step seven are most often neglected in problem solving? Why is that?

3. Your positive attitude is a valuable asset. Imagine that you were making an advertising brochure selling yourself as a problem solver. What personal strengths would you stress? What have you learned through applying the concepts of this book that should be included? What problem-solving skills do you feel comfortable exercising?

4. Discuss areas of growth that are yet needed in your life to become a skilled problem solver. Together, think through a workable plan to continue to grow in this area.

NOTES

CHAPTER 1

[1]James 1:2.
[2]*Webster's New Collegiate Dictionary* (Springfield, Mass.: Merriam Co., 1959), 174.
[3]Harvey Seifert and Howard J. Clinebell, Jr., *Personal Growth and Social Change* (Philadelphia: Westminster Press, 1969), 167–168.

CHAPTER 2

[1]Elliott D. Landau, Sherrie Epstein, and Ann Stone, *Child Development Through Literature* (Englewood Cliffs: Prentice-Hall, 1972), 156.
[2]Ibid., 157.
[3]Ibid., 158.
[4]Edward Ford, *Why Marriage* (Niles, Ill.: Argus Communications, 1974), 73.
[5]Em Griffin, *The Mind Changers* (Wheaton: Tyndale House, 1976), 6.
[6]John Quesnell, *Marriage: A Discovery Together* (Notre Dame, Ind.: Fides Publishers, 1974), 29.

CHAPTER 3

[1]A. W. Tozer, *Knowledge of the Holy* (New York: Harper and Row, 1961), 9.
[2]Colossians 1:13.
[3]Genesis 39:2.
[4]Genesis 39:23.
[5]Genesis 45:8–9.
[6]Hebrews 12:11.

CHAPTER 4

[1] Ephesians 4:12–14, emphasis added.
[2] Ephesians 5:25–27.
[3] Robert Wieder, "Winning At The Game of Business," *Success* (May 1984): 18.
[4] J. Allan Peterson, ed., quoted in *The Marriage Affair* (Wheaton: Tyndale House, 1971), 313.
[5] James 1:2.
[6] James 1:3.
[7] R. C. H. Lenski, *Interpretation of the Epistle of Hebrews and the Epistle of James* (Minneapolis: Augsburg Publishing House, 1966), 527.
[8] 2 Corinthians 1:3–6 (Phillips).
[9] Lenski, *Interpretation of Hebrews and James*, 524.
[10] William Barclay, *The Letters of James and Peter* (Philadelphia: Westminster Press, 1976), 42–43.

CHAPTER 5

[1] T. M. Gregory, "Peace," *The Zondervan Pictorial Encyclopedia of the Bible*, Merrill C. Tenny, ed., Vol. 4 (Grand Rapids: Zondervan Publishing House, 1975), 667.
[2] Galatians 5:22.
[3] 2 Thessalonians 3:16, emphasis added.
[4] Romans 5:1, 2.
[5] Acts 10:36, Ephesians 6:15.
[6] Isaiah 32:17, 18.
[7] John 14:27.
[8] Galatians 5:22.
[9] Philippians 4:7.
[10] Ephesians 2:1–10.
[11] Ephesians 2:14.
[12] John 16:33.

CHAPTER 6

[1] Romans 8:31.
[2] Romans 8:32.
[3] Psalm 23:1.

⁴Matthew 7:11, see also 6:28–33.
⁵Philippians 4:19.
⁶Romans 8:33.
⁷Romans 8:35.
⁸Romans 8:37.
⁹Genesis 12:10–20.
¹⁰Genesis 13:1–18.
¹¹Genesis 16:1–16.
¹²Genesis 22:1–14.
¹³Romans 4:21.
¹⁴Jeremiah 2:13.
¹⁵Tony Walters, *Need: The New Religion* (Downers Grove, Ill.: Intervarsity Press, 1986), 12.

CHAPTER 7

¹James 4:1.
²Maxie Dunnam, Gary Berbertson and Everett Shostrom, *The Manipulator and the Church* (Nashville: Abingdon, 1968), 15.
³Ibid., 19.
⁴Philippians 2:6–7.
⁵Philippians 1:23–25.
⁶Hebrews 11:25–26.
⁷Matthew 22:36–37.
⁸Philippians 2:14–15.
⁹John 13:34–35.
¹⁰Philippians 2:3–4.
¹¹Matthew 22:37–40.

CHAPTER 8

¹1 Kings 1:28–40.
²1 Kings 3:5.
³1 Kings 3:7–9
⁴1 Kings 3:10.
⁵Job 12:13.
⁶Psalm 104:24.
⁷1 Corinthians 1:24.
⁸Revelation 7:12.

[9]Daniel 2:20–23.
[10]Daniel 2:47.
[11]Ephesians 4:17–24.
[12]James 3:13–18.
[13]Tozer, *Knowledge of the Holy*, 66.
[14]Ecclesiastes 7:19.
[15]1 Corinthians 2:9–12.
[16]Jeremiah 25:3–7.
[17]Daniel 2:23
[18]Colossians 3:16.
[19]Tozer, *Knowledge of the Holy*, 66.

CHAPTER 9

[1]Luke 15:11–24.
[2]Galatians 5:22.
[3]John Powell, *Why Am I Afraid to Love?* (Chicago: Argus Communications, 1967), 4.
[4]Psalm 145:8.
[5]Powell, 5.
[6]1 John 4:19.
[7]Lawrence Crabb, *The Marriage Builder* (Grand Rapids: Zondervan, 1982), 108.

CHAPTER 10

[1]A. W. Tozer, *The Pursuit of God* (Harrisburg, Pa.: Christian Publications, 1958), 99.

CHAPTER 11

[1]Ephesians 4:14–16.

CHAPTER 12

[1]Romans 12:20.

CHAPTER 13

[1]Proverbs 15:18.

[2]Proverbs 15:1.
[3]Proverbs 16:28.
[4]Proverbs 22:10.
[5]Ephesians 4:31–32.
[6]Robert Bolton, *People Skills* (Englewood Cliffs: Prentice-Hall, 1979), 221.
[7]Ibid., 217.

CHAPTER 14

[1]John Powell, *The Secret of Staying in Love* (Niles, Ill.: Argus Communications, 1974), 74.
[2]Luke 6:45.

CHAPTER 15

[1]Ralph Nichols and Leonard Stevens, Quoted in *Are You Listening?* (New York: McGraw-Hill, 1957), 49.
[2]David Johnson, *Reaching Out* (Englewood Cliffs: Prentice-Hall, 1972), 210.
[3]Proverbs 15:13.
[4]Bolton, *People Skills,* 210, 211.
[5]Proverbs 20:5.
[6]Bolton, *People Skills,* 220.
[7]David Johnson and Frank Johnson, *Joining Together,* Second edition (Englewood Cliffs: Prentice-Hall, 1982), 304.

CHAPTER 16

[1]John 4:29.
[2]James 3:2.
[3]Proverbs 16:24.
[4]Bolton, *People Skills,* 7.
[5]Jesse Nirenberg, *Getting Through to People* (Englewood Cliffs: Prentice-Hall, 1963), 2–13.
[6]Ibid., 8–9.
[7]Proverbs 11:9, 12.
[8]Proverbs 12:18.
[9]Proverbs 10:32.
[10]Proverbs 13:3.

[11] Proverbs 21:23.
[12] Norman Wakefield, *Listening* (Waco, Texas: Word Books, 1981).

CHAPTER 17

[1] Psalm 32:8.
[2] Bolton, *People Skills*, 240.
[3] *Bits and Pieces* (January 1985): 1–3.